PACKET COMMUNICATION

Robert M. Metcalfe

Foreword by Vinton G. Cerf,
with RFC #62 by D. C. Walden
and RFC #89 by Robert Metcalfe

Peer-to-Peer
Communications, Inc.

This book is
Volume I

of

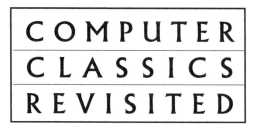

COMPUTER CLASSICS REVISITED

Peter H. Salus, *Series Editor*

Upcoming Books in the Series:

Code and Commentary on the UNIX Operating System (V6)

Planning the ARPANET: The BBN Reports for 1969

*Before the ARPANET: RFCs 1-10 + "A Study of Computer
Network Design Parameters"*

Packet Communication
Copyright © 1996 Robert M. Metcalfe. All rights reserved.

Computer Classics Revisited Series
Series Editor: Peter H. Salus

Published by Peer-to-Peer Communications, Inc.
P.O. Box 640218
San Jose, California 95164-0218, U.S.A.
Phone: 408-435-2677
Fax: 408-435-0895
E-mail: info@peer-to-peer.com

Cover Design: Mayapriya Long, Bookwrights of Charlottesville, VA
Production: Bookwrights of Charlottesville, VA
Printing: Data Reproduction Corporation, Rochester Hills, MI
Cover art of Janus Head from *A Dictionary of Classical Antiquities, 2nd Edition: Mythology, Religion, Literature & Art.* From the German of Dr. Oskar Seyffert. Revised and Edited, with Additions, by Henry Nettleship, M.A. and J.E. Sandys, Litt.D., London: Swan Sonnenschein and Company, New York: MacMillan and Company 1891.

Printed in the United States of America
2 3 4 5 6 7 8 9 10

ISBN 1-57398-033-1

Peer-to-Peer Communications offers discounts on this book when ordered in bulk quantities. For more information, or to receive a current catalog, please contact the publisher at the address above.

Peer-to-Peer Communications' books are distributed to bookstores worldwide through International Thomson Publishing. In the U.S.A. and Canada, contact ITP at
    7625 Empire Drive
      Florence, KY 41042.
For addresses of ITP offices in other countries, contact Peer-to-Peer.

Contents

Series Overview

I believe that there are lessons to be learned from the past: The technical and scientific paths that lead to where we are aid us in seeing where we can go.

Something over three years ago I began working on *A Quarter Century of UNIX*. After it appeared (in 1994), I wrote *Casting the Net: From ARPANET to Internet and Beyond*, which appeared in 1995.

While doing the research for these volumes, I came to realize that many of the most important documents were so ephemeral that I was constantly begging for copies of them. For example, the vast majority of the early Arpanet Requests For Comments (RFCs) could not be located in even the best technical libraries. Moreover, virtually none of the first 500 (!) have ever been available online.

Many of these documents are of more than merely historical interest, and are passed on from hand-to-hand in increasingly blurry copies: fourth and fifth generation versions are treasured by their owners.

The unavailability of these documents forces technologists to retry solutions where the answers are already known.

I decided to try to find a cooperative publisher for some of these works and, luckily, was able to get in touch with Peer-to-Peer. The result is this volume, the first of the "Computer Classics Revisited."

It contains contributions by three of the individuals who wrought the bases for the LANs and the Internet of today. The meat of the volume is Robert M. Metcalfe's Harvard dissertation, *Packet Communication*.

Together with Metcalfe's conception of the Ethernet, *Packet Communication* shows us how the ideas of packet radio could ameliorate the problems of congestion. And without these ideas we would have neither the LANs nor the Internet of today. Toward the outset of his dissertation, Metcalfe mentions Dave

Walden's RFC 62 as a "road not taken," perhaps to our loss. Walden's work—done at BBN, where he spent most of his career—has never been available online, nor has it been published. I am grateful to him for allowing me to reproduce it as an appendix. Vint Cerf was one of the creators of the TCP/IP suite; he was the founding president of the Internet Society; moreover, *he was there* at UCLA in September 1969 when the first ARPANET host was connected. His Preface gracefully and seamlessly weaves Metcalfe's and Walden's work into the fabric of contemporary networking. I have interjected an earlier work of Metcalfe's, RFC 89 (January 19, 1971) as an appendix: it will give the reader a taste of where the ARPANET was when there were under 20 hosts.

As a bonus, Metcalfe has kindly reread his dissertation and supplied his commentary to his work of over 20 years ago. In that time the Matrix has grown from about 150 users to over 35 million. Cerf and others predict well over 500 million in another decade.

Peter H. Salus
Boston
Winter 1996

Series Foreword

ORIGINS

The history of computer communications shares with all histories of technology the common thread of information sharing and building upon the work of pioneers. Peter H. Salus offers to those who wonder what the technical thinking must have been like "back then" a substantive opportunity to read original source material and form opinions based on information unfiltered by the views of intermediaries and commentators.

Robert Metcalfe and David Walden were two very influential participants in the development of packet communication technology. Walden was one of the key developers of the ARPANET system and Metcalfe, after an epiphany late in 1972 on reading work by Norman Abramson on the ALOHANET and a subsequent visit to Hawaii, returned to invent the Ethernet with David Boggs.

Metcalfe's experience in Honolulu was based on a two-channel radio system called the ALOHANET which had been developed by Norman Abramson at the University of Hawaii, under support from the Advanced Research Projects Agency which funded the original ARPANET effort in 1968/69. Metcalfe recognized that the potential congestion of a randomly shared channel could be ameliorated by having the competing sources "back off" in some exponential fashion if they detected "collisions" which indicated excessive demand. It was this "trick" which made the Ethernet such a successful design. As his dissertation clearly shows, Metcalfe participated in the ARPA Packet Satellite effort and was exposed to the ARPA Packet Radio efforts. The competitive use of common radio channels was a hot topic in the early 1970s and Metcalfe's comments, analyses and references illustrate the cutting edge thought of that time. I found Figures 4-2 and 4-3 of particular interest (packet satellite and packet radio) because they illustrate the common thinking of the period that these radio-based networks would more or less attach to the ARPANET as a kind of access net, plugging directly into the ARPANET IMPs.

One of the more profound concepts Metcalfe put forward was the notion of "best efforts, thin wire" communication. At the time, interprocess communication was a key idea and Metcalfe strongly and persuasively argued that the protocol architecture should treat all processes as if they were "remote, mutually suspicious" and able to communicate only over "thin wires" (rather than sharing memory - a "fatter" kind of communication mode). "Best efforts" referred to the idea that the basic communication system was not necessarily reliable and that external methods beyond the best efforts of the basic system were needed.

By the time that Metcalfe's thesis was actually published (December 1973), a framework for internetting had begun to emerge using gateways interposed between the various packet networks as platforms for interpreting internet TCP packets. In September 1993, Bob Kahn and I prepared a note for a meeting of the International Network Working Group (INWG) in Brighton, England at the University of Sussex. Walden prepared a lengthy memorandum expressing his ideas for advancing beyond the NCP model. Many of these ideas found fertile ground in the revised paper Bob Kahn and I wrote for publication in the IEEE Transactions on Communications in May 1974 outlining our ideas for Internet protocols. Metcalfe participated in the fleshing out of the details of these ideas the following year, while he and Boggs were also building the first of the Xerox Ethernets at the Xerox Palo Alto Research Center.

A team of graduate research students at Stanford, including Yogen Dalal, Carl Sunshine, Richard Karp, James Mathis and Ronald Crane, tackled the detailed fleshing out of the basic structure during the summer and fall of 1974 and the first detailed specification emerged in December, 1974, as RFC 675.

Coincidentally, Bob Metcalfe and Bob Bressler were graduate students working on Project MAC at MIT in the 1970-72 period. Metcalfe built the IMP interface to the PDP-10 and Bressler wrote the ARPANET Network Control Program (NCP) for that particular machine. Bressler later joined Bolt Beranek and Newman where he worked with Walden and many others on the ARPANET.

Walden, together with other members of the BBN team including Jerry Burchfiel, Bernie Cosell, Ray Tomlinson and Bressler, had given a great deal of thought to the basic notions of inter-process communication. In the TELNET protocol, these pioneers introduced the fundamental negotiating paradigm: WILL

WON'T DO DON'T which became a kind of mantra for all TELNET extensions that came afterwards.

Walden laid the groundwork for RFC 62 in the period before 1970 while the ARPANET was still in early development. He had been thinking about interprocess communication in time-sharing systems and was interested in exploring alternatives to the connection-like NCP design. Walden and Bressler stressed simplicity and flexible rendezvous ideas for interprocess communication. The idea was that processes would "meet" (rendezvous) at locations (hosts) in the network. Finding each other in a distributed environment was a major element of their view of interprocess messaging and the Message Switching Protocol (MSP) represented a well thought out example of their ideas. Interestingly, the MSP never quite caught on, perhaps in part because of the long history of connection-oriented work in the Network Control Protocol (NCP) but also because uncertainty in the maximum length of messages led to the need for increasingly connection-like mechanisms as message sizes increased.

These source documents make fascinating reading from the perspective of an Internet grown global in the intervening 22 years. It is hard to believe that so many of the ideas found in these early contributions have found purchase in the successful systems of today - and even more interesting to discover how much other territory was covered in the uncertain search for the future. The path always looks clearest when viewed in reverse but as readers may plainly see, there was a forest of ideas out there which obscured the future until it actually happened.

Vint Cerf
Camelot
August 1995

Ruth, Bob, and Bob Metcalfe at 1973 Harvard Commencement

Retrospective

Computing archaeologist Peter Salus says that thousands of people will want to read this book, *Packet Communication*, my 1973 doctoral dissertation about the Aloha and Arpa computer networks. Even if you know technology and are interested in history, why would you want to read a 23-year-old doctoral dissertation? Because, say Peter and I, this controversial dissertation is about Alohanet and Arpanet, it was written at the Massachusetts Institute of Technology, it was rejected at the eleventh hour by Harvard University, it was developed further at the Xerox Palo Alto Research Center, and then it was accepted begrudgingly by Harvard, all just in the nick of some pretty historic times. Turns out that 1973 was a very big year for inventions in computer networking, and this dissertation was smack in the middle of it.

Packet Communication was the last thing written before the invention of the Ethernet (CSMA/CD) local-area network and the Internet (TCP/IP) wide-area network. Now, 23 years later, if you believe the most optimistic estimates, the round number of computers on Ethernets and the round number of users on the Internet are both 50 million -- a big number which may also be written five times ten to the seventh. So, this dissertation is part of a story about some early paving of the, yes, Information Superhighway. It's about Alohanet becoming Ethernet. It's about Arpanet becoming Internet. How can you possibly resist reading this stuff?

Who Really Invented Ethernets and the Internet?

Now, in all the fuss about this dissertation, no one has ever disputed that I wrote it. Who cares? But, hey, the Information Superhighway, Iways, the Net,

Cyberspace, or whatever are now suddenly BIG TIME. Lots of people are hungry for the truth about who really invented Ethernets and the Internet which connects them. Might you be expecting me to claim credit? It's tempting, but these days it's out for white males of European descent to have invented anything. These days it's more correct to go along with the obviously silly notion that nothing was ever actually invented by anyone -- there were just a lot of people standing around gently on one another's shoulders. I don't buy all this exactly, but for some of the shoulders I stood on, see the lengthy acknowledgements section of the dissertation itself.

Anyway, all I needed to do, said Peter Salus, was read my damned dissertation one more time and write this retrospective. I saw at once that this would give me a chance to take some pot shots at my critics and to say I told you so. Peter would get it published. And your captivation about what happened during networking's big invention year would drive you to read it. How nice, thanks to Peter and you, for some vindication on my 50th birthday.

Peter suggested we bundle in Arpanet pioneer Dave Walden's related historic paper on networking protocols. I agreed. Then I suggested we also bundle in an early Arpanet memo of mine, showing just how arrogant I was even before inventing Ethernet and founding 3Com Corporation. Peter agreed. Then Peter suggested that Vint Cerf, Father of the Internet, write our foreword. Vint agreed. And now I'm suggesting that it would do you some good to read it all. Well, how about it?

In the Beginning There Were No Personal Computers

Let me begin recounting in short how this dissertation got written, what happened right afterward, and what's (not) been learned in the 23 years since. Keep in mind that I have not tried to be balanced and fair here. If someone else has a different view, let her write her own retrospective.

First, you must understand that while this retrospective was written on a Macintosh connected into the Internet through an Ethernet, *Packet Communication* was not. I know it's hard, but you've got to understand that in 1973 there were no personal computers. I want you to sit down for a while and think about this, get it clear in your head: no personal computers.

Nitpickers will argue that there were PCs in 1973, but no reasonable person today would recognise them as such. IBM's monopoly was still stifling innovation in computing, but then again Microsoft had not yet taken over that role, so things weren't all bad, but still, get this: no personal computers.

In 1968, while an undergraduate at MIT, I persuaded Digital Equipment Corporation (DEC) to lend me a PDP-8S minicomputer to explore the application of small computers in education. Being the size of a large microwave oven, the PDP-8S might have been a personal computer, but keep in mind that its user interface was a teletype, its mass storage was paper tape, and even Bill Gates couldn't afford to buy one, especially since the founding of Microsoft was still seven years in the future.

Anyway, my PDP-8S was small enough so that in 1968 I became the first person in history (as far as I know) to have his or her computer stolen. Imagine all the explaining I had to do to my patrons at DEC when they came to pick it up. Turns out, this was good practice for much later, like in 1981, when I raised a million dollars of venture capital for 3Com by promising The Year of the LAN in...1982.

Computers in 1973 included many beauties such as the IBM 1401, 1620, 7094, 360/91, CDC 6600, Univac 1108, GE 645 running Multics, SDS 940, Sigma 7, DEC PDP-1, PDP-8, PDP-11 running Unix (even way back then), and my favorites the PDP-6 and PDP-10 running MIT's Incompatible Time-Sharing System, DEC's TOPS-10, and BBN's Tenex. It's funny now that computers in those days had widely varying word lengths including 12, 16, 18, 24, 32, 36, 37, 60, and 128 bits. The 8-bit byte was still very much a coming thing.

Another funny thing about 1973 is that there were literally hundreds of respectable programming languages. All of them were approximately as good as the one we have 23 years later, C++, which is to say not very good at all. Sure, compilers run a whole lot faster these days, but that's mostly due to advances in semiconductors, not programming languages.

The top technology crusade in 1973 was not yet personal computing, but interactive time-sharing on minicomputers. A mere foot soldier in the crusade, I got caught up in explaining to people that the batch processing of punched cards was fine and all, and that mainframe-controlled Selectric typewriters were indeed a vast improvement, but that the future would be even more interactive, and that 30-character-per-second echoplex teletypes attached to time-shared minicomputers were the wave of the future.

Arguing daily for interactive time-sharing was very good practice, it turns out, for later crusades to advance packet switching, personal computers, local-area networks, and now, with considerably more sophistication, the World Wide Web on the Internet. Oops, please disregard that mention of the Web, as I'm trying to get you back into the mood of 1973, when only Doug Engelbart at SRI had any real idea about multimedia hypertext, Bill Gates was in high school, and Marc Andreessen was in diapers.

Don't Tell Harvard They Forced Me to Invent Ethernet

In 1969, I received my draft deferment, graduated from MIT, and headed up the river to Harvard for graduate study on an NSF traineeship. By 1970, I had my masters degree, lost my NSF support, hated Harvard, and needed a job while finishing my doctoral research. An MIT fraternity brother, Dave Burmaster, was at the time working back down the river for Professor Lick Licklider at MIT Project MAC (now the Laboratory for Computer Science). Dave told me Lick was hiring and introduced me to Al Vezza, Lick's right hand man. Al soon had me building hardware to connect Project MAC's DEC PDP-6 to an Interface Message Processor (Imp) on the Advanced Research Projects Agency Network (Arpanet), forerunner of the Internet. By the way, the Arpanet Imp interface I built for Al remained in service at MIT for the next 13 years, and I now have it hung on my office wall.

By 1971, I was a prominent graduate student in the growing Arpanet community and, intending to receive my Ph.D. in 1972, I started writing my Harvard dissertation about how the Arpanet worked. In early 1972, I submitted a draft to Harvard, started making the rounds of institutions that hire newly minted Ph.D.s, got nine job offers, convinced my wife to give up her MIT job to move with me to Xerox Parc, invited my parents to Harvard's commencement in June, and began preparing for my oral thesis defense. In May, while packing to move to an apartment we had rented in Palo Alto, I went up the river to Harvard for my thesis defense ... and promptly failed. Gulp. My doctoral committee told me what I had written was not theoretical enough -- too much straightforward engineering and not enough original computer science. So, my hatred of Harvard was not unrequited.

Granted, the long-lost first draft of *Packet Communication* had many problems, not the least of which was that I had insisted on typing it into a computer through a new process known as word processing. The computer was a time-shared mainframe and you typed into it with a 2741 -- a mainframe-controlled Selectric typewriter. In those days mathematical symbols were usually handwritten with India ink onto manually typed manuscripts. I was too stubbornly modern for manual typing and India ink, so I used only mathematical symbols that a 2741 could regurgitate. This meant, as you will see in the dissertation, that I did not use Greek letters in my formulae where most mathematicians do. To this day I think that my using word-processable Arabic letters for variable names was half the reason my thesis was initially rejected and later pooh-poohed at certain major research universities by important queuing theory professors named Leonard Kleinrock.

While we're nitpicking letters, let me explain why I write Arpa instead of ARPA and Parc instead of PARC. Two reasons. First, I think capitalizing an acronym indicates that it is pronounced as letters, as in IBM, DOD, TCP/IP, and CSMA/CD. Arpa is invariably pronounced as a two syllable word, not A.R.P.A. Parc is a one syllable word, not P.A.R.C. Second, in Ascii cyberspace, capitalizing entire words indicates SHOUTING. So, I avoid shouting ARPANET! Sadly, my editors at InfoWorld would change it to ARPAnet, which is way too UGLY for me. And there's a glimpse of how much of a nitpicker I am.

The parents of this nitpicker were stunned by the news of my (I hoped) delayed graduation from Harvard. After absorbing their disappointment, I screwed up the courage to call my boss at Xerox Parc, Bob Taylor. Bob said come to Palo Alto anyway and finish the dissertation there. God bless Bob Taylor.

Discovering Alohanet on Steve Crocker's Couch

When I got to Xerox Parc in July 1972 sans Ph.D., I was given the job of putting Parc on the Arpanet much as I had done for MIT Project MAC. I did the straightforward engineering on another Arpanet hardware interface and got it all working. Meanwhile, I was informally serving Arpa in facilitating the transfer of packet switching technology. On my frequent trips to Washington, I usually stayed at the home of Arpa program manager and friend, Steve Crocker, and slept on a convertible couch in his living room. This turned out to be really important, so listen carefully.

One night at Steve's in late 1972, jet lagged as usual, I could not get to sleep. So I got up and went looking for something to read. I found a 1970 AFIPS Conference Proceedings -- AFIPS being the American Federation of Information Processing Societies, now defunct. With the big blue book back in bed, I ran across a paper by Professor Norm Abramson of the University of Hawaii in which he analyzed the performance of the Alohanet packet radio network. I not only stayed awake through the whole paper, but thanks to MIT Professor Alvin W. Drake, I understood the mathematics, and disagreed with them.

Actually, what I disagreed with was Professor Abramson's queuing model, which assumed that Alohanet had an infinite number of users each of whom would go on typing even when getting no response. Being myself a network user, this didn't seem quite right to me. And looking for something theoretical with which to finish my Harvard dissertation, I reworked Abramson's model under more realistic assumptions.

To make a long story short, I noticed that Abramson's math did not take into account the parameters of the Alohanet's retransmission process. I noticed that the performance of an Alohanet depended on these parameters. And I noticed that if these parameters were controlled according to traffic, the instability of the Alohanet, which Abramson had modelled, could be eliminated. Bingo.

My parents drove up to Boston in June 1973 to watch me get my Ph.D. from Harvard. MIT Project MAC, not Harvard, published my Harvard Ph.D. dissertation in December 1973, as its Technical Report 114.

Zero to 50,000,000 Ethernet Connections in 22 Years Flat

Just as I was finishing *Packet Communication*, my pals at Xerox Parc gave me the job of designing a network for a new personal computer, the Alto, forerunner of almost everything we hold dear in computing today. For one thing, the new network had to connect hundreds of Altos, one under each desk throughout our building. Just this simple thought was at the time revolutionary. Even the term "local-area network" (LAN) was about eight years in the future (circa 1981). We called them "local computer networks," which I still like better, but have to admit that the acronym doesn't pronounce as well.

The new local network had to carry documents to our planned laser printer, the first laser printer (that I know of). I later wrote the operating system and networking protocols for this printer, which spit out a page per second at 500 dots per inch. Do the sums. Our new network had to run at megabits per second if there was to be any chance of keeping this printer busy.

On May 22, 1973, after much consultation with colleagues, including especially Butler Lampson and Chuck Thacker, I typed a memo describing the high-speed local network we would be building. In that memo I renamed our Alto Aloha Network to EtherNet. Soon I started writing it Ethernet, and maybe someday ethernet will become a household word.

That June I teamed up with Dave Boggs. We spent the next two years building a 100-node Ethernet. After filing for a patent on Ethernet, our paper appeared during July 1976 in the Communications of the ACM (Association for Computing Machinery).

To make another long story short, I worked on Ethernet at Xerox until 1979. Then I began work on making Ethernet an open industry standard and on starting up 3Com Corporation to exploit that standard. In 1982, 3Com became the first company to develop Ethernet for the IBM Personal Computer -- there are now more than a hundred such companies. In 1983, PC Ethernets started selling like hotcakes. In 1984, 3Com went public, and I was suddenly a millionaire on paper. By the time I retired -- some say ejected -- from 3Com in 1990, we had over 2,000 employees and $400 million in annual sales.

By now there are 50 million computers on about 5 million Ethernets worldwide. Not bad for straightforward engineering.

Incidentally, since retiring from 3Com, I've become an oddity. I'm a wealthy journalist. Well, a trade journal pundit anyway. I write a weekly column in the Internet section of InfoWorld. And I give an occasional speech, my new speciality being the "terminal keynote." I like to speak last at a conference, summarizing it for hard-core attendees, getting in the last word on all the big shots who have blown through the conference on their busy schedules. Not a bad life, really. Next stop: Pulitzer Prize.

How the Internet got Invented

During the summer of 1973, while insisting that friends call me Dr. Bob, I continued my involvement with the Arpanet by attending a seminar organized by Professor Vint Cerf down the street at Stanford University. We met to work out a second-generation protocol for the Arpanet. Cerf and Bob Kahn built on that seminar to devise what would become the Transmission Control Protocol and Internet Protocol (TCP/IP). In parallel, I continued work inside Xerox on a similar protocol called the Parc Universal Packet (Pup). Pup later became the Xerox Network System (XNS), shipped in 1980. XNS was later transformed into IPX/SPX, which is the protocol now widely installed in Novell NetWare networks. I've heard it said that Pup added the IP to TCP/IP, but let's work that out some other time.

Just to be clear, since I often make fun of how credit for inventions gets allocated, the TCP/IP Internet was invented and persistently pursued for 20 years under the leadership of Vint Cerf and Bob Kahn. Cerf and Kahn are often and properly acknowledged for their magnificent accomplishment. Let me do so again: Congratulations and thanks, Vint and Bob.

This humble doctoral dissertation explored issues that had to be confronted in the design of TCP/IP. Among these issues were optimal packet and message sizes, message fragmentation and reassembly, flow and congestion control, naming, addressing, and routing, store-and-forward delay, error control, and the texture of interprocess communication. I was fortunate to be among the many who Cerf and Kahn drew into confronting these and other issues during the design of TCP/IP. For my contributions, Cerf and Kahn generously acknowledged me in their historic TCP/IP paper published in 1974. My overlapping work on Pup and XNS at Xerox, and later the commercial implementation of TCP/IP at 3Com, put me in the thick of early Internet developments, but not so much in the thick as to put my contributions in a class with Cerf and Kahn's. I hope, all kidding aside, this is clear.

Also in 1980, TCP/IP became a standard of DOD, and in December my merry band at 3Com shipped the first commercial implementation of TCP/IP.

In 1983, making yet another long story short, the Arpanet was upgraded to run TCP/IP and became the Internet. The Internet grew rapidly after that until really exploding in 1993 with the introduction of Mosaic for the World Wide Web. There are now somewhere between 5 and 50 million users of the Internet, depending on how you count and who you believe, but it's safe to say that TCP/IP has caught on. Cerf and Kahn should be, have been, and will many times again be honored for inventing TCP/IP and more so for sticking with the Internet for 25 years. Cerf is now widely known as the Father of the Internet -- he'll have to work that out with Kahn.

Remembering Amy Jill Blue

In *Packet Communication*'s acknowledgements section you will read about "my meta-sponsor, the irrepressible, the irresistible," my then wife Amy Jill Blue Metcalfe. Amy Jill Blue was MIT's draft counselor when I showed up in her office during January 1968, at the height of the Vietnam War. We eloped in May and, after putting up with my working round the clock on the Arpanet at MIT, she moved west with me to Xerox Parc. And then, after putting up with me working round the clock on Ethernet, she finally suggested in late 1975 that we amicably dissolve our marriage.

Amy soon thereafter remarried and had two beautiful children (as if there is any other kind). Before seeing her children grown, however, Amy was diagnosed with inoperable brain cancer, which she fought off for a year. The day she died I wondered what kind of God would let a thing like that happen.

A moment of silence, please, to remember Amy.

Toward a Calculus of Store and Forward Packet Switching

Now, on to the dissertation itself. The first thing *Packet Communication* attempts is a calculus for store-and-forward packet switching. In retrospect, 23 years later, this attempt seems in parts wrong and in other parts obvious.

The dissertation is wrong, in retrospect, where it focuses on transmission errors, then approximately one bit in error out of every hundred thousand bits transmitted. Since then, transmission systems have improved steadily, error detection and correction have been perfected, and most of the errors that packet switching systems have to worry about are in computer hardware and software, mostly software.

The dissertation is obvious, in retrospect, where it calculates in various ways that the delay through a packet switching system is proportional to $N*P/C$, where N is the number of store-and-forward routing hops, P is the packet length in bits, and C is the circuit speed in bits per second. The mathematics behind $N*P/C$ are nothing sophisticated -- probably wasn't rocket science even in 1973 -- but this simple formula, or something close to it using Greek letters, is central to the design of Ethernet, TCP/IP, ATM, Fast Ethernet, and many other packet switching systems.

How Alohanet Led to Ethernet

Of course the dissertation's mathematical consideration of a controlled Aloha channel for packet radio led directly to the invention of Ethernet. So, in principle, I should be grateful to Harvard for insisting that my Ph.D. dissertation be more theoretical. But, frankly, I don't feel grateful.

Anyway, despite numerous mentions of Abramson's Alohanet work in this dissertation and in almost all Ethernet materials since, I've heard repeatedly over the years that, because it uses randomized retransmissions, Ethernet is merely an Alohanet rip-off. Well, these critics may have a point. Ethernet is just exactly like Alohanet. Except Ethernet does not have a central controller like Alohanet's Menehune. Except Ethernet has a single transmission channel with two-address packets instead of Alohanet's two channels with one-address packets. Except Ethernet, unlike Alohanet, has carrier sense to avoid most collisions and to carry long packets efficiently. Except Ethernet, unlike Alohanet, has collision detection so as not to waste bandwidth. Except Ethernet has retransmission back-off control for channel stability, like Alohanet didn't. And except finally that Ethernet runs at millions of bits per second over cable within buildings, while Alohanet ran at thousands of bits per second over radio among the Hawaiian islands. So, with these few exceptions, sure, Ethernet is exactly like Alohanet.

Abramson's Alohanet technology has turned out to be very important in the subsequent development of digital packet communication technology. Important in the development of Ethernet, as I keep admitting, and also important in the development of satellite communication systems. Where Alohanet technology has over these last two decades failed grossly to meet expectations is in the development of terrestrial packet radio -- no Dick Tracy wrist-top computers yet. This is fine with me. I don't see advancing communication technology as a way to make it possible for us to be away from our families and friends even more than we are now. My advice after all these years is, Wire up your home and stay there.

Much of the math in *Packet Communication* and subsequent work on Ethernet was cross-checked with computer simulations. Boggs and I simulated everything to be sure we were on the right track. Unfortunately, we promptly threw all our simulation printouts away. Ever since, we have had to contend repeatedly with the criticism that Ethernet behaves poorly, just like Alohanet.

Even today, I still run into people who believe either that Ethernet does not really work all that well, or as Boggs is fond of saying, "Ethernet works well in practice, but not in theory." Well, excuse me, but Ethernet, as first studied through Alohanet in *Packet Communication*, works well in both theory and practice. Two decades of queuing theory graduate students have worked on improving Ethernet, and in the end the most they get is a percent or two here and there, and then only after assuming something unrealistic like there are an infinite number of users or that Ethernet standards can be changed willy nilly.

Best-Efforts, Thin-Wire Interprocess Communication

My favorite part of *Packet Communication*, now, is the closing essay on best-efforts, thin-wire interprocess communication. There I argued that all elements of a distributed system should be accessible as if [not local but] remote from one another, and that components of a network should all view one another with mutual suspicion.

In retrospect, I don't think we've yet figured this out. Our distributed systems still lack resilience. We still have inadequate security. Our programming languages still don't systematically check for errors, still don't systematically report, and rarely recover from error conditions. We still suffer too many transient, unexplained, and unrecoverable network failures, which is not to say exactly that the Internet is to this day a house of cards.

You often read that the Internet grew out of the Arpanet, which was developed by DOD to survive thermonuclear war. This goal for packet switching was mentioned in Paul Baran's pioneering writings at the Rand Corporation circa 1964. However, nobody I ever talked to working on the Arpanet thought about how it would keep on routing even if several of its centers were to experience a simultaneous rise in temperature of 30 million degrees.

If surviving thermonuclear war was a goal of Arpanet research, then looking at today's Internet you can see that the goal was not nearly achieved. For example, the Internet couldn't even survive the announcement of a not-guilty verdict in the trial of O.J. Simpson -- the Internet was unavailable to many people that entire day.

You should see the email I get for predicting that the Internet will suffer catastrophic collapse(s) during 1996, leading to a more robust Next Generation Internet. It's a good bet.

Save Us From the Telephone Monopolies

The Arpanet described in *Packet Communication* was an internet of dozens of minicomputers, typically PDP-10s running at less than a million instructions per second, connected in what would later be called LANs of maybe four nodes at 300Kbps, and interconnected nationwide at 50Kbps. Today we have tens of millions of computers in the Internet. Each of these computers is maybe 100 times faster than a PDP-10 and costs maybe a hundredth the price.

There has been a lot of progress in computing since 1973 in the fiercely competitive computer industry. LANs were invented, standardized, and have proliferated, again in a fiercely competitive environment. For example, in 1981, I sold Ethernet interfaces for $5,000. In 1996, Ethernet interfaces are on sale for as little as $19 each in packs of 10. Now that's progress.

On the other hand, we have the regulated telephone monopolies. I led the tour for 10 telephone company executives at the first International Conference on Computer Communications (ICCC) during October 1972 in Washington. Having edited the book of Arpanet demo scenarios for ICCC -- an early Internet for Dummies -- I was asked to show these pin-stripers around, despite my still being a bearded graduate student.

During the demo, for the one and only time at the ICCC, the Arpanet Imp in the Hilton Hotel crashed for a few minutes. I looked up, embarrassed, and found all of my telco executives doing the last thing in the world I would have expected them to do. They were smiling. I was crushed. They were relieved that the Arpanet had crashed. This meant to them that digital data packet switching was no real threat to the world of analog voice circuit switching that they understood and, more importantly, had a monopoly on. They would make it to retirement unscathed.

Since 1972, the regulated telephone monopolies have underperformed the competitive computer industry. Now we are to the point that the half-hearted efforts of the telcos to upgrade their networks to carry digital data are the limiting factor in the advancement of computing and communications, slowing our entry into the Information Age. The telco monopolies and their regulatory regime, including the Federal Communications Commission and 51 state public utilities commissions, must now be completely dismantled, bulldozed, and replaced with a competitive environment that will drive down costs and spur technological advance. Customer premises equipment and long distance services have been successfully demonopolized, and now we have to break the monopolies of the local telcos. This much I have learned in the 23 years since *Packet Communication* was written.

The Embarrassment of Incestuous Traffic

You've probably heard that electronic mail was a totally unexpected major use of the Arpanet. Indeed. But, there was another totally unexpected Arpanet phenomenon, which I in particular find hilarious.

Arpanet Imps -- early routers -- counted packets as they passed through en route to various destinations. And so we got to looking at the numbers each month, watching Arpanet traffic grow and who was sending how many packets to whom. Among the numbers was a major embarrassment, which we just subtracted out and tried not to report. It was the count of packets which came in from one host computer connected to an Imp and went out, not cross country like we were building the Arpanet to do, but to another host computer connected to the same Imp. We called such intra-Imp traffic "incestuous." Now you have to remember that there weren't all that many host computers in the world back then. Having several in close proximity was rare, even at a university research lab. So we thought of incestuous traffic as odd -- just debugging traffic which we Arpanet promoters, I mean researchers, could not take credit for carrying.

Of course, as time went on, much to our annoyance, incestuous traffic grew, further polluting our packet counts. People in the same building were proving too lazy to carry mail down the hall to their colleagues and were instead sending intra-building email. IMAGINE! Little did we know then that we were seeing what would much later be called LAN traffic.

Today, the vast majority of TCP/IP traffic is what used to called incestuous. Using very round numbers, there are now roughly 50 million computers on 5 million Ethernets. Of these, 500,000 are registered as TCP/IP networks, of which 50,000 let some of their traffic out onto the Internet. So, roughly speaking again, while the Internet backbone might be carrying 15 terabytes per month, this is only one millionth of the 15 exabytes per month that the world's Ethernets could carry -- almost all traffic is now incestuous.

By the way, the lesson to draw from these round numbers is that even miniscule changes in the mix of traffic between LANs and WANs can have dramatic effects on Internet loading. This leaves the Internet vulnerable to transient outages when waves of previously-incestuous LAN traffic flood it from time to time.

I Did It, So Can You

Wrapping up, I'll ask again, What's the point of reading *Packet Communication*? No, it won't teach you how to do anything immediately useful, like programming in HTML. But, if you're interested in history, and in seeing how things actually happen, and especially in seeing how information technologies get invented, and even more especially in seeing how such technologies get proliferated, then Peter Salus and I think that this book is an important data point for you.

Thanks to Peter Salus, and Dan Doernberg at Peer-to-Peer Communications, for thinking this book worthy of publication. Thanks also to Mayapriya Long and Chris MacIntosh for pulling it all together. And thanks to you, in advance, for reading it.

My secret hope, dear reader, is that this book will contribute to your seeing more clearly that you can invent something and make it big. If I could, you can, so please do. Meantime, don't let the bastards grind you down.

Bob Metcalfe
Kelmscott Farm, Maine
Winter 1995-96

TIMELINE

1945 World War II Ends

1946 ENIAC built; Metcalfe born in Brooklyn, New York

1947 Founding of the Association for Computing Machinery

1955 In 4th grade, Metcalfe decides to study EE at MIT

1959 In 8th grade, Metcalfe builds calculator with relays

1964 Metcalfe enters MIT

1968 Metcalfe and Amy Blue marry

1969 Metcalfe graduates MIT as electrical engineer, enters Harvard

1970 Starts work on Arpanet at MIT Project MAC

1972 Ph.D. thesis on Arpanet rejected at eleventh hour by Harvard

1972 Left MIT for the Xerox Palo Alto Research Center

1972 Arpanet demo at first ICCC

1973 *Packet Communication* accepted by Harvard

1973 Metcalfe writes Ethernet invention memo at Xerox Parc (5/22)

1973 Metcalfe attends Vint Cerf's TCP/IP seminar at Stanford

1973 *Packet Communication* published by MIT project MAC (December)

1975 Microsoft founded

1976 Ethernet paper, Metcalfe and Boggs, published in CACM

1979 Metcalfe leaves Xerox to pursue entrepreneurial ambitions

1979 Ethernet standardization started with Gordon Bell

1979 Metcalfe founds 3Com Corporation

1980 Metcalfe and Robyn Shotwell marry

1980 3Com ships first commercial version of DOD standard TCP/IP

1981 IBM ships first Intel-Microsoft PC

1982 Ethernet standard agreed; 3Com ships PC Ethernet

1984 Apple Macintosh shipped; 3Com IPO

1987 Julia Metcalfe born, destined for MIT Class of 2007

1989 Maxwell Metcalfe born, destined for MIT Class of 2009

1990 World Wide Web demonstrated by Tim Berners-Lee

1990 Metcalfe out of 3Com, $400 million sales, 2,000 employees

1993 NCSA Mosaic for the World Wide Web by Andreessen, Bina et al

1995 Ethernet and Internet might both have hit 50,000,000 users

1995 San Francisco's Candlestick Park renamed 3Com Park

1996 *Packet Communication* republished by Peer-to-Peer

1997 Conference Chairman, ACM97: The Next 50 Years of Computing, San Jose

1998 25th anniversary of the invention of Ethernet

MAC TR-114

PACKET COMMUNICATION

Robert Melancton Metcalfe

December 1973

This research was supported by the Advanced Research
Projects Agency of the Department of Defense under ARPA
Order No. 2095 which was monitored by ONR Contract
No. N00014-70-A-0362-0006.

Massachusetts Institute of Technology

Project MAC

Cambridge, Massachusetts 02139

Synopsis

This report develops a theory of packet communication; it analyzes uses of computers in digital communication systems and examines structures for organizing computers in highly communicative environments. Various examples from existing computer networks, including the ARPA Computer Network and the ALOHA System, are used to motivate and substantiate analysis of (1) store-and-forward packet communication, (2) broadcast packet communication, and (3) distributed interprocess communication.

In a taxonomy of computer communication techniques, we first distinguish the two basic modes: circuit-switching and packet-switching. Next, we take packet switching techniques and distinguish those most applicable to point-to-point media (e.g., telephone circuits in the ARPANET) from those most applicable to broadcast media (e.g., radio in the ARPANET Satellite System and the ALOHA System).

In 1964, Paul Baran and others, then at the RAND Corporation, published an eleven volume series of technical reports titled "On Distributed Communications" which marks for us the beginning of modern history for the analysis of so-called "store-and-forward" computer communications networks <Baran>. Later, when ARPA began planning what was to become the ARPANET, three major areas of store-and-forward network theory were identified: (1) topological design, led by Howard Frank at Network Analysis Corporation, (2) system modeling and performance measurement, Leonard Kleinrock, UCLA, and (3) store-and-forward switching node design, Frank E. Heart and Robert E. Kahn, Bolt Beranek and Newman, Inc. Our work in the analysis of store-and-forward packet communication is most closely related to that of Kahn, Crowther, and McQuillan at Bolt Beranek and Newman, who, with their intimate knowledge of the IMP and the ability to guide IMP development with theory, have made considerable sense out of IMP operating statistics <Kahn3, Kahn4, McQuillan>.

Synopsis

In our analysis of store-and-forward packet communication, we specify a representative "feedback-correction protocol" for achieving reliable communication over a noisy channel (between store-and-forward packet-switching nodes). We calculate the "total effective capacity" of communications using the feedback-correction protocol. We use several simple error models to derive expressions for the capacity-maximizing packet size. A plot of theoretical effective capacity versus packet size shows that ARPANET effective capacity is insensitive to variations of packet size above 1000 bits. We show that what we call "hop-by-hop" acknowledging feedback-correction offers lower packet transfer times than "end-by-end" acknowledging in a store-and-forward network with non-negligible retransmission probabilities. We derive an expression for optimal node spacing in a store-and-forward network. And, we show how a store-and-forward node converts limited capacity (i.e., bit rate) into delay and how this store-and-forward delay supports the use of message disassembly in the ARPANET.

Radio, on the other hand, is a broadcast medium; a radio transmitter generates signals which can be detected over a wide area by any number of radio receivers. As one might expect, the application of packet communication techniques to radio has led to novel system organizations of a kind different from those of point-to-point transmission media.

With his first, simple model of the "classical ALOHA system", Abramson derived the "ALOHA Result" linking channel throughput and traffic in an asynchronous time-division multiplexing (ATDM) radio system; his analysis assumes infinite-source Poisson packet arrivals and omits the details of randomized retransmission <Abramson1>. Our reconsideration of Abramson's model (1) introduces a finite source model of packet arrivals (user blocking) to better account for the behavior of interactive terminal users in a loaded system, (2) considers the effect of exponentially distributing retransmission intervals, and (3) extends the analysis to obtain the distribution of user block times (i.e., transmission delays).

In recent work by Hayes and Sherman, the delay characteristics of the ALOHA system are compared with those of two other ATDM techniques, namely the Polling and Loop systems <Hayes>. But, again, they model packet arrivals with an infinite-source Poisson process; the same is true of Pack's consideration of ATDM using general results from his analysis of an M/D/1 queueing system <Pack>.

Synopsis

Roberts discovered that a "slotted" ALOHA channel could support twice the throughput of an unslotted channel <Roberts3>; in further analysis of ALOHA systems, we develop a discrete-time model of a slotted ALOHA system, once again bringing into account user blocking and randomized retransmission, deriving the block time mean and variance, and then, additionally, discovering "retransmission control" as a technique for achieving acceptable performance and stability over a wide range of system loads, even well into saturation <Metcalfe9>. Where our analysis considers exponentially and geometrically distributed retransmission intervals, Binder, in subsequent analysis, derives results for the uniform distribution <Binder>. Where our analysis studies an ALOHA system in steady state, very recent work by Lu uses first order homogeneous linear difference equations to get a dynamic description of ALOHA system state <Lu>.

Computer communication is both communication <u>using</u> computers and communication <u>among</u> computers. In the first sections of the report we analyze certain techniques for the application of computing in communication; in the final chapter, we turn to consider a philosophy of communication in computing -- we turn to consider structures for organizing computers in highly communicative environments.

A recurring problem in the development of the ARPANET has been the coordination of remote processes. Any one of a number of existing schemes for interprocess communication might have been expected to offer itself as a ready solution, but, the fact is, the basic organization of ARPANET interprocess communication -- a general HOST-HOST protocol -- was long in coming and troublesome when it arrived. At the time of the Network Working Group's decision to adopt the current "official" HOST-HOST protocol, two specific proposals were considered: one based on connections <Crocker1> and the other on messages <Walden>. The earlier proposal, based on connections, was chosen, we believe, because connections, much more than messages, resemble structures in familiar, centralized computer operating systems.

We believe, in retrospect, that Walden's proposal would have been the better choice -- that the underlying structures of ARPANET interprocess communication should be modeled, not after the centralized computing systems they join, but after the distributed packet-switching system they use. ARPANET experience leads us to suggest that there are valuable distinctions to be made between (1) <u>centralized</u> interprocess communication techniques as often employed within computer operating systems and (2) <u>distributed</u> interprocess communication techniques as required in computer networks. These distinctions bring us to propose that even the latest plans to develop a message-based distributed interprocess communication system for the ARPANET, especially plans for floating "ports" and generalized "rendezvous" <Bressler1>, are not extreme enough in their departure from techniques used in centralized computing systems.

We propose that so-called "thin-wire" strategies for interprocess communication be used more generally within and among computer systems because thin-wire interprocess communication (1) has a clarifying effect on the management of multiprocess activity and (2) generalizes well as computer systems become more distributed. We further propose that so-called "best-efforts" strategies be used more generally because best-efforts interprocess communication (1) takes fullest advantage of the potential for error recovery found in highly error-prone distributed environments and (2) encourages the economic distribution of reliability mechanisms in large systems.

The thrust of our proposal is in opposition to that most often offered by those studying organizations of distributed computing systems:

> All elements of a distributed system should
> be accessible as if <u>local</u> to one another.

By arguing that best-efforts thin-wire interprocess communication should be more generally applied, we propose:

> All elements of a distributed system should
> be accessible as if <u>remote</u> from one another.

Acknowledgements

This report comes after three years of research during which I have benefitted immeasurably from associations with many people in and around the ARPA community. The following text is littered with pointers (e.g., <Roberts2>) into a rather large bibliography whose purpose is to credit those who have contributed to my work and to provide material for those wishing to dig deeper.

I thank my Harvard thesis advisors, Thomas A. Standish and Jeffrey P. Buzen, for their support in the development of ideas for this report; thanks to Thomas E. Cheatham and George H. Mealy for their efforts as my thesis committee members; thanks to J.C.R. Licklider, Lawrence G. Roberts, and Robert E. Kahn for inspirational guidance; thanks to my cohorts at Project MAC including Albert Vezza, Gregory F. Pfister, Howard R. Brodie, J. Pitts Jarvis III, Sue Pitkin, Michael A. Padlipsky, and Allen L. Brown, and thanks to Butler W. Lampson, Howard E. Sturgis, Charles Simonyi and Nilo Lindgren at Xerox PARC, for review and discussions of report drafts; and thanks to Jacquelyn Southern and Janet K. Farness at PARC for picking up where others left off.

My work was supported in part by Project MAC, an MIT research project sponsored by the Advanced Research Projects Agency, Department of Defense, under the Office of Naval Research. My research has benefitted either directly or indirectly from ARPA'S support of the MIT Dynamic Modelling/Computer Graphics PDP-10, Multics, MATHLAB, the MIT-AI PDP-10, the Stanford Research Institute's Augmentation Research Center, the USC Information Sciences Institute PDP-10, Bolt Beranek and Newman, and the ARPANET at Xerox PARC. Additional support has come from Robert I. and Ruth C. Metcalfe of Brightwaters, New York, the Harvard Center for Research in Computing Tech-

Acknowledgements

nology, Harvard University, the Xerox Palo Alto Research Center, and the National Science Foundation under its Traineeship Program.

But then there's my meta-sponsor, the irresistible, the irrepressible, Amy J.B. Metcalfe.

Bob Metcalfe
Xerox PARC
Palo Alto, California
July 1973

Table of Contents

Table of Contents

Table of Contents

List of Figures

Introduction

"Electronic communications technology has developed historically almost completely within what might be called the circuit
switching domain. Not until the last decade has the other basic mode
of communication, packet switching, become competitive. ... most
of the experiments with packet communications have been under-
taken by computer scientists, and it is not even generally recognized
yet in the communications field that a revolution is taking place. ... it
is generally written off as a possibly useful new twist in communications utilization, and not recognized as a very different technology
requiring a whole new body of theory."

-- Dr. Lawrence G. Roberts

This report develops a theory of what we, as computer scientists, call "packet
communication". Current understanding of computer communication justifies
only the simplest of theories, and ours, while fragmented and tentative, is appropriately comprehensible and readily applicable.

What Is Packet Communication?

To begin with, a packet is not a circuit. Circuits are the units of allocation
predominant in traditional electronic communication systems. When you make
a telephone call, for example, the telephone system establishes an electrical
path between you and the person you're calling by joining available telephone
cables -- circuits -- end-to-end. To complete your "connection", the telephone
system's exchanges -- switching nodes -- allocate cable-miles in the form of

circuits and maintain this allocation for the duration of your call. Thus, in circuit-switching, we say, circuits are allocated to carry connections.

Packets, like circuits, are units of allocation in communication systems; unlike circuits, packets have only recently become appropriate for electronic communication. When you mail a letter, for instance, the mail system moves it from post office to post office in various bags and bundles -- packets -- through successive way stations, repeatedly using the address you specified to route the letter toward its destination. To deliver your "message", post offices -- "switching nodes" in telephone terminology -- allocate man-hours and mailbag-miles to the various packets in which your letter is contained en route to its intended receiver. Of course, depending on the sizes of the messages being carried, a packet may contain many messages, or only parts of a message, or possibly many parts of many messages. Thus, in packet-switching, we say, packets are allocated to carry messages.

In this report we are concerned with the application of packet-switching in digital electronic communication and with the impact of this application on the organization of computing systems. We are concerned with computers in two ways: first, as components in building electronic packet-switching systems, and, second, as the benefactors of the communication provided. When we say "computer communication", we indeed mean both (1) communication using computers and (2) communication among computers. Whereas "packet communication" was first intended to refer to the use of computers in certain novel organizations of communication systems, we have come to apply the phrase more generally, namely to include computing techniques peculiarly appropriate to the highly communicative environments provided by these novel organizations.

The Advantages of Packet Switching

In pure circuit-switching, the making of a connection requires a number of distant switching nodes to piece together a continuous path from end to end; and, for the life of the connection, its constituent circuits are dedicated to carrying a conversation. For a very short conversation, the effort required to set up its connection is large in contrast to the number of bits transmitted; for a conversation with a substantial fraction of inactive periods, the number of useful bits transmitted is small in contrast to the number that might have been transmitted were the constituent circuits fully utilized. Circuit-switching makes poor use of communication facilities when the conversations being carried are either short or very "bursty".

In pure packet-switching, on the other hand, the communication system does not dedicate circuits to set up connections; rather, the messages which form a conversation are injected individually at the exact moment of their readiness. Because there is no connection setup to amortize over a conversation, short conversations are not seriously disadvantaged relative to long ones; because a packet-switching system allocates its resources to messages rather than conversations, the inactive periods in one conversation can be used to support other conversations. Packet-switching makes good use of communications facilities when the conversations being carried are either short or very bursty.

The principal disadvantage of packet-switching is, of course, that each packet -- each message in a conversation -- is transmitted with a complete specification of the communication desired (e.g., destination, source, size, sequence number, priority). For long and continuous conversations, the repetition of these specifications in each packet can be costly; it would be better to use the specifications once to set up a connection and to send streamlined messages through dedicated circuits.

"Pure" circuit-switching and "pure" packet-switching are only the extreme ends of a spectrum of system organizations. From one end, with high-speed electronics, circuit-switching can become much more flexible than our description above might suggest: circuit switching is often done very quickly by electronic (rather than human or mechanical) switching systems, and the multiplexing of circuits among many conversations is certainly a highly refined science <ESS>. From the other end of the spectrum, to get some of the efficiencies of circuit-switching, packet-switching systems can be compromised to dedicate various resources to connections: connection-like structures are often built into or on top of packet-switching systems so that they can economically carry either connection or message traffic <McKenzie1>.

Distributed computing systems have generated growing pressure for packet-switching. Computer "conversations" have become shorter and burstier, especially with the spread of so-called "interactive" computing. Circuit-switching systems have been greatly improved toward providing the responsive communication required by distributed interactive computing networks, but this communication is probably best provided by packet-switching systems. While computers have been demanding electronic packet-switching, they have also been making it possible.

In the following chapters we draw upon existing packet-switching computer communications networks -- most notably the ARPA Computer Network -- to substantiate our theory of packet communication. For those who are somewhat familiar with the history of interactive computer time-sharing, our use of the ARPA Network in discussing packet communication may evoke strong associations; the role of the ARPA Network in packet communication is reminiscent of the role of early time-sharing systems, CTSS for example, in interactive computing <Roberts, Roberts2, Samuel>. In both cases we find a strong commitment to dynamic resource allocation; to computing resources in CTSS and to communication resources in the ARPANET. And just as the apparent expense of time-sharing has long been attacked by the advocates of batch processing, so too has the apparent expense of packet-switching been attacked by the advocates of circuit-switching; in both cases, again, it is the continued decline of the cost of computing which has made it possible to utilize other resources more effectively, to squander computer cycles and baud miles for some greater good.

How to Read the Report

One can, of course, read this report directly from front to back, but a prior knowledge of its tree-like branching structure is helpful. We have already distinguished two fundamental modes of electronic communication, its two major branches: circuit and packet. The report deals only with the packet communication branch. Under packet communication, we distinguish communication using computers from communication among computers. Chapters 2, 3, 4, and 5 are devoted to, roughly, the use of computers in communication, while chapter 6 examines communication among computers. Under communication using computers, we distinguish between techniques based on point-to-point and broadcast communication media, studied in chapters 2 and 3 and in chapters 4 and 5, respectively. For each of the two media considered, we devote a chapter to existing techniques and a chapter to analysis. If the preceding linear description of our bifurcate chapter organization is confusing, one can, of course, read this report directly from front to back.

Those who are already familiar with "packet communication" should read chapters 3, 5, and 6, three chapters in which our original contributions are concentrated. For those who wish to go beyond a full reading of the report and its instructive appendices, a sizable bibliography has been provided. The literature surrounding various subjects to be discussed, particularly in the more analytical sections, is summarized immediately before the relevant text and then referenced where appropriate.

Opened Questions

A number of important questions are opened in the following chapters, both in packet communication theory and in the closely related theory of distributed computing. Many of our own answers suggest new questions; they await actual operating environments and careful measurements of loaded systems <Cole> for validation.

For instance, our examination of the behavior of individual store-and-forward nodes fails to consider difficult questions concerning their interconnection. Some work has been done in this direction using queueing theory < Kleinrock, Kleinrock1, Zeigler> and network flow theory < Frank>, but we remain dissatisfied (1) with the simplifying assumptions often used to obtain clean analytical results and (2) with the short cuts often employed to escape prohibitive combinatorics. What is needed, we are convinced, is a readily applicable calculus of communications elements (e.g., circuits, memory, processors) like that of the network theory of resistors, capacitors, and inductors.

The report touches on the question of fundamentally different organizations of communication, i.e., circuit versus packet, sequential versus random-access, and centralized versus distributed. Satellites, ground radio, and cable television are only three of the unusual computer communications media with which subsequent theories of the organization of communications must deal <Roberts2>. What is needed is a theory much like that missing also from the field of transportation. We will need to have theories for mode selection, mixture, and, possibly, hierarchies of modes. We might imagine having an understanding of when a person should take a moving sidewalk, to a car, from a bus, to a train, through an airport, to a space shuttle. Similarly we will need to know whether a packet should go over a VLF channel, to a telephone, through a UHF channel, to a satellite, over a microwave link, through a laser, to a TV station. Of particular interest will be a theory that organizes the use of connection-oriented and message-oriented switching techniques at appropriate levels in computer communication systems.

Introduction

Missing from much of the work in computer communication is a consideration of user utility functions and demand distributions. A critical input to packet size selection, for example, is a distribution of user communication requirements, i.e., message sizes. Who knows what the sizes of people-people, computer-computer, or process-process communications would be were they not constrained somewhat arbitrarily by the communications systems which carry them? It is likely that each application will have its own performance requirements; a most important problem to be solved is that of building general-purpose communications systems which benefit from the complementary requirements of the various applications to be supported. It will be important that careful consideration be given to assessment of inputs to design, as well as to design itself.

The open questions in distributed computing are numerous. How should one organize accounting and access control in a distributed computer utility <Gruenberger, Saltzer, Kahn1, PCI>? In the ARPA Computer Network, accounting and access control are handled (if at all) locally, each service computer having to assume the responsibility for protecting its resources from intrusion over the network. It is uncertain whether distributed accounting and access control systems will require new organizations of computing activity <Kahn1>. It may be that (1) the inherent separateness of actors in a distributed environment and (2) the required explicitness of their cooperation will make accounting and access control a natural part of distributed computing.

We need to consider "naming" in widely distributed computing systems. It was first suggested to us by D. Austin Henderson (MIT) that carefully chosen naming conventions -- a theory of names -- would be needed in dealing with program-manipulable name spaces of the size required in world-wide computing environments. Even in the relatively small and sparse ARPA Network, name manipulation has already become a problem <Bhushan4, Bressler, Postel1>.

To utilize the potential of distributed computing systems we will need to develop techniques for managing cooperating concurrent processes. Control structures for programming languages <Fisher, Thomas, Prenner> have been advanced, but it appears that many basic questions are still unanswered. In practice, the development of protocols for remote, asynchronous processes has been informal, despite the fact that race conditions and deadlocks abound. The result is that existing protocols are a patchwork of seemingly arbitrary sequencing rules <Postel1>. Jonathan B. Postel (UCLA) has suggested, and we agree, that some sort of graph theoretic (e.g., Petri Net) formalization of ARPANET protocols will prove fruitful <Postel2>. A generalization of approaches to program correctness will be required for use in distributed and highly parallel contexts <Habermann>.

The ARPA Network has developed the need for formerly isolated systems to interface to the outside world. The obstacles to this interface have often been of the kind where a simple standard would have made things easy. Computer communication will continue to provide pressure for standards in computing as the importance of cooperation and compatibility grows relative to that of competition and contrariety. In particular, it is essential that standards be developed for terminals, data representation, and file organization so that many of the needless incompatibilities that artificially partition the population of computer users can be removed <Anderson, Hostel, Michener, Crocker3, Harslem1, Bhushan, Bhushan1>.

The ARPANET

The Advanced Research Projects Agency (ARPA) Computer Network (ARPANET) has been an important vehicle for studying the efficacy of packet communication techniques, both in the utilization of digital data communications facilities and in the closely related development of distributed computing systems. To support the analysis of the next chapter, we will briefly explain what <u>we mean</u> when we say: The ARPANET is a geographically distributed, message-switching, store-and-forward, high data rate, highly connected, modular, computer communications network. Rather than discussing the ARPANET in its full generality, we focus only on store-and-forward packet-switching using computers and point-to-point communication media,

Recent years have witnessed an accelerating demand for <u>computer communications</u> <Brown, Gruenberger, Kittner, Parkhill>. Through communications, the organizers of computing systems have found new ways of structuring resources and distributing services. Through computers, the organizers of communications systems have found new ways for providing information flow in an increasingly interconnected world.

Consider how communication influences computing. For example: ARPA research in the development of computing resources has led to the construction of the ILLIAC-IV and the UNICON Laser Memory. These devices are representative of a class of large scale computing facilities which cannot easily be justified without a workable plan for providing access to large, distributed user populations.

For another example: Basic research in the application of computing resources has led to undertakings requiring a broadly based integration of previously separate people and technologies. For example, ARPA's success in Automatic Programming <Balzer1, Cheatham1, MAC>, Climate Dynamics, and

Speech-Understanding <Newell> will depend on its success in providing for computer-enriched cooperative interaction <Licklider> among distributed research teams.

Now consider how computing influences communication. Investigations of computer communications systems have progressed slowly for over a decade <Baran, Kleinrock1, Marill>. The technologies which support computing and communications have only recently advanced to provide performance characteristics near those required for effective, interactive computer communication. Submicrosecond processors, memories, and communication circuits, at costs far below those five years ago, make it possible to consider wide use of computers in communication: aiding human operators in routine functions; replacing slower and less reliable mechanical switching systems; and extending services in novel applications never before possible <ESS, Roberts2>.

In moving toward a design for a computer communications system for the ARPA computer research community, three characteristics of the community were influential. First, the ARPA community spans the nation. Second, the emphasis in the ARPA community is on interactive computing. And, third, the computing resources in the ARPA community are diverse and autonomous. Emphasis on these characteristics is essential to any understanding of why or how the ARPANET differs from other computer communications networks <Farber, Abramson, Rutledge, Roberts2>. The basic structure and design parameters of the ARPANET are derived from these characteristics.

ARPANET Descriptors and Parameters

The ARPANET is a geographically distributed computer communication network with, currently, about 6000 miles between its most distant nodes. (See Figure 2-1.) That it is nationally (if not globally) distributed is significant in fixing the parameters of its communication circuits and in organizing its installation and maintenance subsystems.

The ARPANET is a message-switching network permitting up to 8095 bits per message <Heart>. It transacts, not with circuits as in the case of telephones, but with messages (i.e., packets) as in the case of mail <Roberts2>. Communicating computers do not dial each other up through the switching system and have conversations, digital or otherwise; they send each other packets of digital data, like letters through the mail. That the ARPA community emphasizes inter-

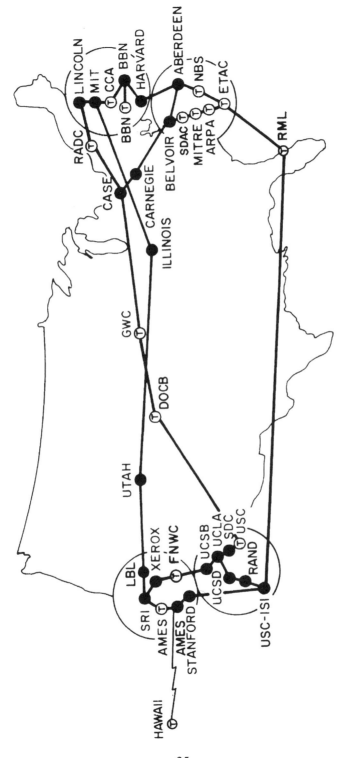

FIGURE 2-1 ARPA NETWORK, GEOGRAPHIC MAP
MAY 1973

25

active computing is reflected in the ARPANET's optimized handling of interaction-sized messages of up to 1000 characters <Roberts>.

The ARPANET is a store-and-forward computer communications network with on the order of 100,000 bits of packet storage per switching node. Its communications computers store messages until assured of their safe arrival at the next node en route to a destination. These communications computers are either (1) Interface Message Processors (IMPs)(BBN1822, Heart> or (2) Terminal IMPs (TIPs) <Ornstein>. That the ARPANET's switching nodes (IMPs) have between 100,000 and 200,000 bits of memory (rather than 1,000,000 or 100,000,000) is evidence that the ARPANET places a premium on responsiveness—short message queues for low delay rather than long queues for high circuit utilization. Switching nodes of previous store-and-forward networks (e.g., DOD's AUTODIN) were often equipped with mass memories (e.g., disks) where messages were queued for minutes, hours, and even days. Long-term message storage is provided in the ARPANET, but not by the switching nodes themselves; such message storage and forwarding is provided through protocols and programs residing in the "HOST" computers joined by the IMP Subnet.

The ARPANET is a relatively high data rate network with circuits carrying, typically, 50 kilobits per second (Kbps). In contrast to earlier networks which often used dial-up 2400 bps or 4800 bps telephone circuits, the ARPANET uses dedicated 9.6, 50, and 230.4 Kbps telephone circuits for the responsiveness and throughput required of effective interactive use.

The ARPANET is a low-delay network guaranteeing less than .5 seconds delay coast-to-coast <Frank1, Heart, Roberts>. Human interactions of the variety normally supported by the interactive time-sharing systems in the ARPA community would be impractical via a communications network with transmission delays on the order of minutes, hours, or days. This low delay characteristic of the ARPANET is the result of (1) the use of relatively small messages, (2) high data-rate circuits, and (3) restricted IMP message storage.

The ARPANET is a highly connected network with, typically, 2 or 3 independent paths between nodes. This minimum two-path redundancy offers reliability of access and increased throughput <Frank>. Though "highly" connected (most networks are 1-connected), the ARPANET is not completely connected, i.e., not all IMP pairs are directly connected by a circuit. (See Figures 2-1 and 2-4.) Rather the ARPANET is connected so as to provide an economic level of communication under loads varying widely in space and time. In contrast to the more familiar loop and star network topologies, the ARPANET's arbitrarily connected, store-and-forward communications subnet offers measured reliability and ease of growth over a wide range of network sizes <Frank>.

Finally, the ARPANET is a highly <u>modular</u> computer communications network. Modularity is a necessity for ARPANET reliability and manageability. The ARPANET is modular in that the IMP Subnet operates independently of the connected computers at ARPA sites <Heart>. The ARPANET is modular in that each of the IMPs and their programs are identical; hardware maintenance and software development are both thereby simplified <McKenzie>. The ARPANET is modular in that its communications protocols are strictly layered. (See Figures 2-2 and 2-3.) The strict layering permits separate teams to work in parallel at many levels of development and supports cleanly defined interfaces among levels of varied purpose <Crocker>.

At the lowest level, the IMP-IMP protocol <Heart> handles transmission error control, message (i.e., packet) traffic congestion control, and packet routing. IMPs detect transmission errors with a 24 bit checksum for each 1000 bit packet and correct errors using an acknowledgment-retransmission scheme <Heart>. The IMP Subnet regulates the entry of messages from HOSTs to control packet traffic congestion and transmission delays <BBN1822, Heart, McQuillan>. Packets are routed through the IMP Subnet using an algorithm which locally minimizes transit time <Frank, Frank1>. IMP-IMP protocol is implemented in software within the DDP-516/316 IMPs.

At the next level up, a widely used "official" HOST-HOST protocol <Carr, McKenzie1> provides a general purpose virtual communications system among

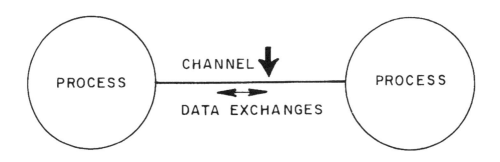

FIGURE 2-2 GENERAL PROTOCOL MODEL

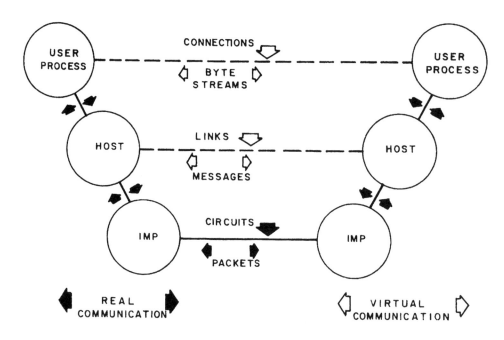

FIGURE 2-3 LEVELS OF ARPANET PROTOCOL

processes on remote computer systems. The "official" HOST-HOST protocol is implemented in Network Control Programs (NCPs) <Newkirk> within HOST computers.

And, at a higher level still, numerous function-oriented process-process protocols <Crocker> support specific ARPANET applications. For example, the widely used TELecommunications NETwork (TELNET) subsystem provides console access to the many interactive computer systems on the ARPANET <Postel>.

The ARPANET Present and Future

As of this writing the ARPANET has grown to over 30 sites and is well on its way toward becoming something of a national utility. There are now over 35 HOST computers and 13 TIPS (i.e., Terminal IMPs) joined by the ARPANET to each other and to a growing community of users <Ornstein>.

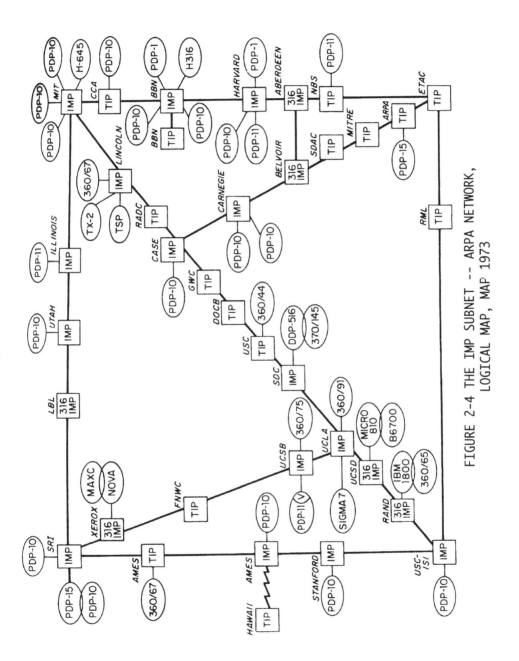

FIGURE 2-4 THE IMP SUBNET -- ARPA NETWORK,
LOGICAL MAP, MAP 1973

The ARPANET

The ARPANET began when the IMP-IMP and IMP-HOST protocols of the communications subnet were delivered by Bolt Beranek and Newman, Inc. <BBN1822, Heart, McQuillan> in early 1970. The ARPA Network Working Group (NWG), an assembly of representatives of ARPA sites, has designed and implemented (1) a general-purpose HOST-HOST protocol <Carr, Crocker, McKenzie1>, (2) a "TELNET" protocol <O'Sullivan, O'Sullivan1, Postel> to allow ARPANET users to log into the various cooperating interactive computers on the ARPANET, (3) an ARPANET file transfer protocol <Bhushan6>, and (4) a remote job service protocol <Bressler2, White>. Work is continuing on (1) a graphics protocol <Michener>, (2) a data computer protocol <Datalanguage>, and (3) a data reconfiguration protocol <Anderson>, among others.

ARPANET development has passed through its initial experimentation/construction phases and is now entering a critical new period in which the facilitation of substantive use must be the dominant activity. There are many problems to be solved. Mechanisms for assuring privacy and security are as yet unknown, especially in the distributed communications environment. The interconnection of widely differing computing systems will generate new pressure for standards. Techniques for charging and accounting in a distributed environment will need considerable study, particularly to make it possible for a non-research management organization to make the ARPANET a self-supporting operation. There are many more problems in the distributed computing environment and its effect on the organization cf computer operating systems <Kahn>.

An important part of the ARPANET's future relates to its smooth transfer to an operational agency for long-term cost-recovery management. Steps are currently being taken to find a suitable management environment for the communications facilities as they now stand. At the same time, private companies are seeking to provide commercial ARPANET-like service and have already filed with the FCC for clarification of their regulatory status <PCI>.

Studies are now in progress toward introducing new communication media at the lowest levels of the ARPANET. The University of Hawaii is already connected into the ARPANET using a point-to-point channel through a synchronous, earth-orbiting satellite; work continues toward building ARPANET Satellite IMPs (called SIMPs) which use that same channel, in a broadcast mode, to provide ARPANET service to stations around the Pacific, from California to Alaska, to Hawaii, and possibly to Japan <Abramson3, Crowther>. It is expected that higher bandwidth terrestrial circuitry will be introduced throughout the ARPANET to continue responsive service at increasing levels of use.

The integration of other networks is also an important part of ARPANET development. Effort is going into the planning of national networks for the United Kingdom, Canada <Manning>, and France, using the ARPANET both as an input to design and as a component in a future world-wide computer communications network. Just as important will be the development of "smaller" networks to complement ARPANET-like facilities in the delivery of computer communications <Abramson, Farber, Roberts2>.

In the next chapter, we focus on the IMP Subnet to analyse store-and-forward packet communication. The reader who is not already familiar with ARPANET IMPs and HOSTs, can find additional background material in Appendices A and B.

Analysis of Store-and-Forward Packet Communication

In a taxonomy of computer communication techniques, we might first distinguish the two basic modes: circuit-switching and packet-switching. Next, we might take packet switching techniques and distinguish those most applicable to point-to-point media (e.g., telephone circuits in the ARPANET) from those most applicable to broadcast media (e.g., radio, to be discussed in the next chapter). With this taxonomy as a context, we now look under point-to-point packet-switching to examine store-and-forward techniques.

So-called "store-and-forward" packet-switching networks, as exemplified by the ARPANET, are growing in popularity. The theories behind such networks are still vague and poorly understood. In this chapter we present a collection of first-order theories of store-and-forward packet communication and extract several rules of thumb which may prove useful in network design.

In 1964, Paul Baran and others, then at the RAND Corporation, published an eleven volume series of technical reports titled "On Distributed Communications" which marks the beginning of modern history for the analysis of store-and-forward computer communications networks <Baran>. Later, when ARPA began planning what was to become the ARPANET, three major areas of store-and-forward network theory were identified: (1) topological design, led by Howard Frank at Network Analysis Corporation, (2) system modelling and performance measurement, Leonard Kleinrock, UCLA, and (3) store-and-forward switching node design, Frank E. Heart and Robert E. Kahn, Bolt Beranek and Newman, Inc.; the development of various theories contributing to the ARPANET is summarized by Frank, Kleinrock, and Kahn in "Computer Communication Network Design—Experience with Theory and Practice"

<Frank1>. Our work in the analysis of store-and-forward packet communication is most closely related to that of Crowther, Kahn, and McQuillan at Bolt Beranek and Newman, who, with their intimate knowledge of the IMP and the ability to guide IMP development with theory, have produced several papers which make considerable sense out of IMP operating statistics <Kahn3, Kahn4, McQuillan>.

Summary

A representative "feedback-correction protocol" for achieving reliable communication over a noisy channel (between store-and-forward packet switching nodes) is specified. The "total effective capacity" of communications using the feedback-correction protocol is calculated. Several simple error models are used to derive expressions for the capacity-maximizing packet size. A plot of theoretical effective capacity versus packet size shows that ARPANET effective capacity is insensitive to variations of packet size above 1000 bits. It is shown that "hop-by-hop" acknowledging feedback-correction offers lower packet transfer times than "end-by-end" acknowledging in a store-and-forward network with non-negligible retransmission probabilities. An expression for optimal node spacing in a store-and-forward network is derived. It is shown how a store-and-forward node converts limited capacity into delay and how this store-and-forward delay supports the use of message disassembly in the ARPANET. And, finally, distance-independence is challenged in its role as an overriding objective of ARPANET design.

Feedback-Correction

Consider the traditional digital communications model: a noisy channel connects the sender and receiver of a potentially infinite bit stream; how can the sender and receiver organize to achieve dependable communication?

In the literature on communications error control we find many methods of introducing redundancy into transmitted data so that errors can be <u>detected</u> through observed inconsistency and <u>corrected</u> by using redundancy in damaged transmissions <Berger, Gorog, Lin, Peterson, Sussman>. The effectiveness of various coding techniques for error control depend on the error characteristics of the noisy channel to which they are to be applied. It has been found, in particular, that because "burst" errors are typical of commonly used communication media (e.g., telephone circuits), the redundancy required to deter transmission errors is significantly less than that required to <u>correct</u> damaged data <Lin, Mitchell, Peterson, Smith>. The computations required to decide if a transmission is in error are typically much less complicated than those required to reconstruct it <Smith>.

When it happens that there is a unidirectional channel from sender to receiver, there is little choice but to use "open-loop" error control techniques requiring high data redundancy and elaborate correction procedures. When the channel connecting sender and receiver is bi-directional, it is possible to use "closed-loop" error control techniques, using per-packet redundancy for error detection only and relying on receiver-controlled retransmission for error correction <Kalin, Lin, Smith>. By making data reconstruction unnecessary, "closed-loop" or "feedback" correction allows transmitted data to be much less redundant and simplifies the computations required for error control.

A particularly simple family of feedback-correction communication protocols has found application in contemporary computer communications systems <Abramson, Farber, Heart, McQuillan, Roberts2>. This family of protocols is based on error-checked packet transmissions, acknowledgments (ACKs), time-outs, and retransmissions: a sender generates a packet of data with sufficient redundancy to reduce the probability of undetected error to an acceptably small number (e.g., one undetected incorrect bit every ten to the twelfth transmitted data bits); the packet is transmitted and stored until an error-checked acknowledgment of its safe arrival is returned from the error-checking receiver; if an error-free acknowledgment fails to arrive within a given time-out period, the sender assumes that the transmitted packet has been lost and retransmits it; and so on forever; the receiver, upon getting a packet, checks to see if it is damaged and, if not, generates an error-checked acknowledgment packet to be returned to the data sender. To guard against packet duplication, a typically trivial sequencing mechanism is used <McQuillan>. There are a number of variations on this protocol which compose the family under study.

A simple feedback-correction communication protocol is more formally and succintly specified in the accompanying flowcharts. Our consideration of a particularly simple, representative feedback-correction protocol began during informal discussions with Steve Crocker (ARPA), Jon Postel (UCLA), and later with presentations by Richard Kalin (Lincoln Lab, now at ADR) <Kalin> and Alex McKenzie (BBN) <Cerf1>.

For simplicity, the start of transmission is assumed to be synchronized and a single-bit sequencing scheme is used for duplicate suppression. Error checking of data packets and ACK packets is assumed to offer a satisfactory level of protection from undetected error. It will be instructive to step through a few scenarios of the cooperation between a sender/receiver pair under this simple protocol. Study the flowcharts, Figures 3-1 and 3-2.

Feedback-Correction Scenarios

First, let us look at a case where everything goes well. The sender (in start state "zero") generates a packet with appropriate state "zero" sequence bit and error-check bits. The packet is transmitted and the sender goes into state "zero" time-out wait. The packet arrives at the receiver where the error-check procedure declares the packet to be correct (i.e., consistent); it is immediately acknowledged with an error-checked state "zero" ACK packet from receiver to sender. The receiver notes that he is in state "zero" and that the newly received packet is a "zero" packet (i.e., in sequence); he includes the new data bits as part of the received data stream. The receiver then puts himself into state "one" to await a state "one" packet. The sender, meanwhile, has received an error-free ACK marked with state "zero" and is assured that the pending, state "zero" packet has been received without error. The sender then moves into state "one" and restarts the cycle by generating a state "one" packet from the data awaiting transmission.

Next, consider what happens when the state "one" packet is found by the receiver to be damaged (i.e., inconsistent, in error) The algorithms for sender and receiver both require that all damaged packets be discarded and ignored. The damaged packet (probably, but not in general necessarily, a damaged state "one" packet) takes the receiver out of data wait and is discarded. The receiver immediately re-enters data wait looking once again for a state "one" packet. The sender, in time-out wait looking for a state "one" ACK, (1) finally times out, (2) retransmits the pending state "one" packet, and (3) falls back into state "one" time-out wait. Eventually, (1) a retransmission of this state "one" packet gets to the receiver undamaged, (2) the packet is acknowledged with a state

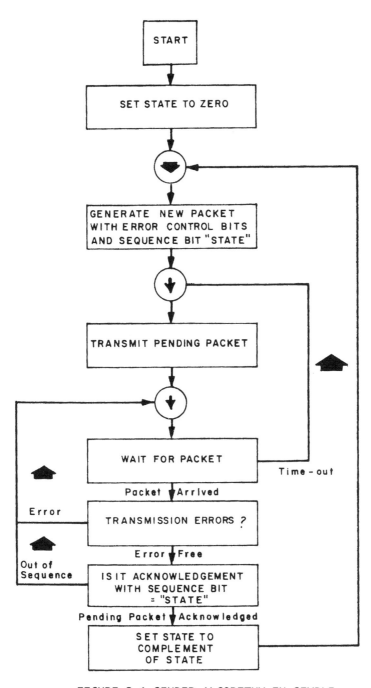

FIGURE 3-1 SENDER ALGORITHM IN SIMPLE
FEEDBACK-CORRECTION

37

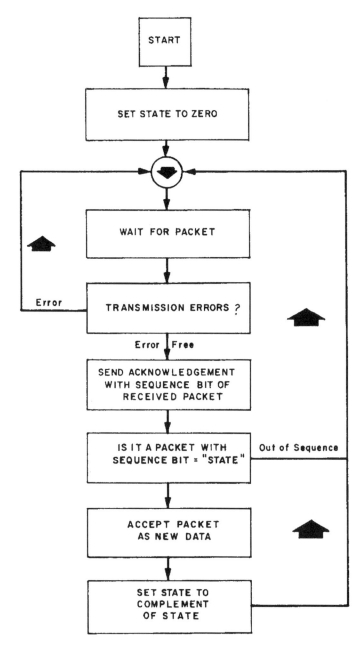

FIGURE 3-2 RECEIVER ALGORITHM IN SIMPLE
FEEDBACK-CORRECTION

"one" ACK, (3) the receiver enters state "zero" in preparation for the next message in sequence, and (4) the newly arrived data is accepted by the receiver as part of the transmitted bit stream.

Next, consider what happens when the state "one" ACK is lost or damaged. If damaged, an ACK will be discarded and thereby lost. If the state "one" ACK is lost, the sender in state "one" will fail to receive the ACK before timing out and thus the pending state "one" data packet will be retransmitted. The receiver, having sent the lost state "one" ACK and now in state "zero", gets the retransmitted state "one" packet successfully (say) and sends a state "one" ACK. The receiver notices, however, that the packet is out of sequence (i.e., a "one" and not a "zero" packet); the duplicate packet is discarded. The ACK generated by this duplicate data packet serves to satisfy the waiting sender and to advance the transmission sequence.

If a state "one" retransmission were to somehow pass its delinquent state "one" ACK on the wires, the protocol would cause the retransmitted state "one" packet arriving at the state "zero" receiver (1) to be acknowledged, (2) to be declared a duplicate (i.e., out of sequence), and (3) to be discarded. The second state "one" ACK, in turn, would arrive at a state "zero" sender and would also be discarded as a duplicate.

This simple protocol is intended to exhibit the basic properties of a family of error control protocols. There are variations on this basic protocol. By adding a negative acknowledgment (NAK) to the protocol in cases where ACK times are very uncertain (a time-out is still required), the transmission of data can be speeded by reducing the time taken by the sender to decide to retransmit a damaged packet. By adding more sequence bits in cases where ACK times are very large, more packets can be pending (i.e., on the line) and the potential utilization of the channel thereby improved. Packet reconstruction schemes (i.e., error correction) can be superimposed on the feedback-correction mechanism to reduce retransmission frequency. Some of these variations are a matter of detail and others are important. For our initial analysis of the properties of the family of protocols, the above mentioned simple representative will be used.

Effective Capacity and Delay

The channel connecting sender and receiver has a given nominal capacity (bit-rate) of C bits per second and a given transmission delay of d seconds. How will the error characteristics of the channel and our simple feedback-correction protocol combine to provide an "error-free" connection between sender and receiver? What will the "effective capacity" (bits per second) and the "effective delay" (seconds) of our virtual connection be, under the proposed organization of channel use?

The error properties of a channel are difficult to characterize and the probability of a transmitted packet arriving in error is undoubtedly a complicated function of time and packet length. Real channels are often subject to a mixture of both random and burst errors <Berger, Kahn2, Lin, Sussman>. For the simple calculations at hand, we (1) fix the independent error probability of a data packet at Lp, (2) fix the independent error probability of an acknowledgment packet at La, and (3) define L ("L" for "Loss") as the probability that an acknowledged packet transmission will fail (i.e., will time out), where:

(Eq. 3-1) $$L = 1 - (1-Lp)*(1-La)$$ $(0 \leq L < 1)$

A successful, acknowledged transmission requires a successful data packet transmission with probability 1-Lp and a successful ACK packet transmission with probability 1-La. L, then, is the probability that something will go wrong with either the data packet or the ACK. L is the probability that a retransmission will be required given that a transmission is attempted.

Let k (a random variable) be the number of retransmissions required for a successful, acknowledged transmission of a data packet under our simple protocol. The event corresponding to k=0 is that in which the first transmission of a data packet leads to its successful receipt and timely acknowledgment (i.e., without need for retransmissions). The probability of the k=0 event is 1-L, by our definition of L. We write Prob(k=0)=(1-L). The event corresponding to k=1 retransmission involves an unsuccessful attempt at an acknowledged data packet transmission, with probability L, followed by a successful attempt, with probability 1-L. The event corresponding to k=1 (i.e. one retransmission) has probability L*(1-L). We write Prob(k=1)=L*(1-L). For k retransmissions, we recognize the geometric distribution:

(Eq. 3-2) $$\text{Prob } (k=i) = L^i * (1-L)$$ $(k \geq 0)$

The mean number of retransmissions per successful transmission is calculated in a straightforward manner leading to Equation 3-3:

40

(Eq. 3-3)   Mean k $= \dfrac{L}{(1-L)}$ $(0 \le L < 1)$

In summary, if the probability of an unsuccessful, acknowledged packet transmission is L, independent of previous attempts, then the mean number of attempted transmissions per successful transmission is $1+(L/(1-L))$.

How long will it take to successfully transmit an acknowledged packet through the channel using our simple feedback-correction protocol? For our calculations, let P be the number of bits per data packet and let A be the number of bits per acknowledgement packet.

The mean time for a successful transmission is now calculated in a straight-forward manner leading to Equation 3-7.

First, we consider the time required for an acknowledged packet transfer without retransmissions. Time zero is taken to be the time at which the sender starts transmission of the data packet. The time taken by the sender to transmit a data packet is P/C seconds -- P bits being transmitted at the nominal channel bit-rate of C bits per second. The sender ends data packet transmission and enters time-out wait at time P/C. Because of the channel transmission delay of d seconds, the receiver begins getting the data packet at time d and has finished receiving it by time (P/C)+d. The receiver takes, say, zero time to error check the packet.

(This assumption is not as restrictive as it looks: d can be adjusted to include checksum computation and modem delay < Crocker2>.) Therefore, the receiver begins sending the ACK packet of length A bits at time (P/C)+d and finishes transmission at time (P/C)+d+(A/C). The sender begins getting the ACK d seconds later and has it in hand and error checked by time (P/C)+ d+(A/C)+d. Thus ends a successful acknowledged transmission cycle, so that:

(Eq. 3-4)   Time $(k=0) = ((P/C)+(2d)+(A/C))$

But how long would an acknowledged packet transfer take if there were errors and retransmissions? If either a data packet or ACK were to be damaged and lost, the sender would be forced to time out and retransmit, thereby delaying successful transfer completion.

A key quantity is the amount of time that the sender will wait before retransmitting -- the time-out, T seconds. We will assume that the sender is what we call an "optimistic" sender, i.e. a sender who is willing to wait (before retransmitting) at least as long as it would take for an ACK to return if all went well. A "pessimistic" sender might retransmit an unacknowledged (i.e., pending) data packet even before an acknowledgment could be expected to arrive. Retransmission pessimism might be motivated by a very high retransmission probability (e.g., $L>(1/2)$) and/or by a desire to utilize an otherwise idle channel <McQuillan>.

Assuming that the time-out parameter T is greater than the acknowledgment time $((2d)+(A/C))$ seconds, then, we get that the time required for an error cycle -- the time by which an error delays eventual successful transmission -- is $(P/C)+T$ seconds, so that:

(Eq. 3-5) $\qquad$ Time $(k=i+1) = ((P/C)+T) +$ Time $(k=i)$ $\qquad$ $(i \geq 0)$

Combining with our expression for Time$(k=0)$, we get:

(Eq. 3-6) $\qquad$ Time $(k=i) = ((P/C)+(2d)+(A/C)) + i* ((P/C)+T)$

Now by knowing the mean number of retransmissions (error cycles) required for a successful acknowledged transmission, we can calculate the mean time required:

(Eq. 3-7) $\qquad$ Mean Time $= ((P/C)+(2d)+(A/C)) + \dfrac{L}{1-L} * ((P/C)+T)$

This mean transmission time can be used as a measure of the "effective delay" across the sender/receiver connection; it is also important in calculating the effective capacity of the "error-free" connection supported by our simple protocol. By "effective capacity" we mean the average sustained rate of error-free bit transfer achievable through a channel. Effective capacity is calculated by taking the ratio of (1) the number of good data bits transmitted per packet, to (2) the mean time of successful, acknowledged packet transmission.

We have defined P as the number of bits per packet, but not all the bits in a packet are data bits. Some packet bits are error control bits (e.g., checksums), others are sequence bits (e.g., our state sequence bit), and still others may be required in more complex communications contexts (e.g., an ARPANET-like switching network) for routing and flow control.

For our purposes, we say that there are S data bits per P packet bits and, more specifically, P=B*(H+S). H (for "Header Overhead" in bits per packet (≥0)) is taken as a constant, per packet overhead, and B (for "Bit Overhead" in bits per bit ≥1)) is taken to be a constant, per bit overhead factor. B is usually 1, but we carry it along as a variable because it extends the model without complicating our calculations. We can now write an expression (using Eq. 3-7) for the effective capacity (in bits per second) of our sender receiver connection:

$$\text{(Eq. 3-8)} \quad \text{EFFCAP} = \frac{S}{((P/C) + (2d) + (A/C)) + \dfrac{L}{1-L} * ((P/C) + T)}$$

Before moving on to simplify this expression, let us examine its structure. The numerator is S alone and we will say that, if data bits are a small fraction of those in a packet (i.e., if S is relatively small, S<<P), then the effective capacity of our connection is <u>overhead limited.</u> Looking at the denominator, we see that a number of terms may dominate in the limitation of effective capacity. If the nominal channel capacity, C bits per second, is so small as to make the P/C and A/C terms large in the denominator, we say that our connection bit-rate is channel <u>capacity limited.</u> If the 2d term dominates, then we say that effective capacity is <u>delay limited</u>. Similarly, a high L causes the retransmission term to grow large making transmission capacity <u>error limited</u>. Improper choice of T in a high error environment could make effective capacity <u>time-out limited.</u>

To achieve maximum effective capacity as calculated above, the sender must have as much data as he wants. If the sender has only finite storage available to him, then he must get additional data from some remote source. Therefore, the sender's ability to push bits through a channel may be limited (further) by his inability to supply them. He may have to wait for bits from another sender, over another feedback-corrected channel, which in turn has a limited effective capacity. In a situation where the sender is limited by his inability to store queued data, we say that the effective capacity of the channel is <u>queue storage limited</u>. We do not consider this effect.

The receiver may not be able to dispense with bits quickly enough to suit the sender and may have to discard (for later retransmission) some correctly received packets for want of buffer storage. We do not consider such effects <Zeigler>. Neither do we consider the effect of variable length packets. These ignored effects should be included in a more comprehensive theory.

When the variance of acknowledgment return times is small relative to the mean, the sender can set his time-out time T at the expected return time (or just above) with little penalty. In that case, the time required for an error cycle (i.e., for a transmission and time-out) is the same as that for a successful data-ACK packet exchange, $((P/C)+T)=((P/C)+(2d)+(A/C))$ seconds.

If the acknowledgment return time has a high variance, then a tight time-out would be less effective, due to the resulting, frequently premature retransmission of correctly received and acknowledged packets. For the following calculations, we assume that the variance is small relative to the mean.

Using the equality $T=((2d)+(A/C))$ seconds, we simplify our expression for effective capacity to:

$$\text{(Eq. 3-9)} \qquad \text{EFFCAP} = \frac{S*(1-L)}{((P/C)+(2d)+(A/C))} = \frac{S*(1-L)}{((P/C)+T)}$$

By collecting terms with an eye toward structure, we get:

$$\text{(Eq . 3-10)} \qquad \text{EFFCAP} = \frac{S}{P} * \frac{1}{(1+(C*T/P))} * (1-L)* C$$

We now see that our calculation of effective capacity for the simple feedback-correction protocol reduces to the product of four factors: (1) an <u>overhead factor</u> (S/P), (2) a multiplexing factor $(1+ (C*T/P))$, (3) an <u>error factor</u> (1-L), and, of course, (4) a pure <u>capacity factor</u> (C).

Having an expression for the effective capacity of a simple feedback-correction retransmission protocol (Equation 3-10), we now examine two ways of improving the <u>total effective capacity</u> (TEC) of communications over the raw channel. First, we sketch how the multiplexing factor $(M=(1+ (C*T/P)))$ leads to a simple revision of the protocol and to a lower bound on the number of packet buffers required for high total effective capacity. Second, we introduce three very simple transmission-error models to study the dependence of total effective capacity on packet size. We demonstrate how total effective capacity might be maximized by some judicious choice of packet size.

Round-Trip Delay and Buffering

Of the factors determining effective capacity (Equation 3-10), the so-called multiplexing factor $(M=(1+(C*T/P)))$ exhibits the highest potential for structure-dependent improvement. Examining the factor more closely, we see that the multiplexing factor corresponds to the number of different packets which might usefully be "on the wires" (pending) at once, due to a non-zero acknowledgment time. C*T is the number of bits which could be transmitted over the raw channel while waiting for an acknowledgment to a previous P bits. M is the number of different packets which could be pending at once and is a function only of the ratio of the number of bits which can be transmitted during an acknowledgment time (C*T) to the number of bits in a packet (P). Our expression for effective capacity, above, is reduced by 1/M because the simple protocol described requires that there be but one pending packet.

A basic revision of the simple protocol, then, would be to use at least M copies of it on a single raw channel. Such a parallel use of separate instances of the simple protocol would require (1) instance identification bits in packet headers and (2) sufficient buffer space at the sender to hold at least M different packets. For the current examination we ignore the details of instance identification. (BBN uses this multiple-instance approach in the ARPANET IMP Subnet <Cerf1, McQuillan>.)

We assume, for a given raw channel with specified nominal bit-rate C, acknowledgment time T, and packet size P, that at least M = (1+(C*T/P)) parallel retransmission sequences are maintained. The total effective capacity (TEC) of the raw channel under this organization is then given by Equation 3-10 with the multiplexing factor removed:

(Eq. 3-11) $TEC = (S/P) * (1-L) * C$ ($0 \leq L < 1$)

Notice that the expression for total effective capacity comprises what we call an efficiency factor, (S/P)*(1-L), namely the ratio of good data bits (S) to the mean total number of bits transmitted per successful transmission (P/(1-L)).

There is a trade-off between packet overhead and multiplexing. It takes extra bits in packet headers to maintain parallel instances of our feedback-correction protocol. The number of extra bits needed for instance identification is the rounded up, logarithm base 2, of M. The number of multiplexing bits (i.e., instance identifier bits) is usually very small relative to the total number of header bits, but not always (e.g., in high speed and high delay satellite communication <Crocker2>).

Channel Errors and Packet Size

Intuitively, we see that if our packet size P is large, then (1) the probability of packet transmission error is large, (2) L is near 1, and (3) the total effective capacity of transmission is reduced significantly by the (1-L) error factor. The channel spends most of its time carrying damaged packets to the receiver.

Recalling that P=B*(H+S), we see that if P is small, then (1) S is near 0, and (2) most of the bits transmitted are header bits which do not contribute to effective capacity. The channel spends most of its time carrying header bits.

It must be, then, that there is some packet size P which maximizes total effective capacity. We now introduce three simple models of the error behavior of a raw communications channel to study the dependence of total effective capacity on packet size.

Linear Error Model. We first assume that our channel is a binary symmetric channel <Lin> with transition probability E; the probability of a transmitted bit being received in error is E, independent of all other bits. The probability of a packet of length P bits being in error (Lp) is therefore:

(Eq. 3-12) $$Lp = 1-(1-E)^P$$

By assuming (1) that the approximated probability of a packet error (E*P) is much less than 1 and (2) that acknowledgments (A bits) are much smaller than data packets (P bits), we use Equation 3-12 and the Binomial Theorem to get a linear approximation of the retransmission probability (L=1-(1-La)*(1-Lp)):

(Eq. 3-13) $$L = E*P \qquad (0 \leq E*P \ll 1, A \ll P)$$

Substituting in Equation 3-11 for P=B*(H+S) and for L=E*P, we get:

(Eq. 3-14) $$TEC\,(S) = \frac{S}{B*(H+S)} * (1-E*B*(H+S))*C \qquad (0 \leq E*P \ll 1)$$

Taking the derivative of TEC(S) with respect to S, setting it equal to zero, and substituting for S with P (P=B*(H+S)), we get P´, i.e., the packet size which maximizes total effective capacity:

(Eq. 3-15) $$P' = \text{SQRT}\left(\frac{H*B}{E}\right)$$ $(0 \le E*P' << 1)$
$(P' = B*(H+S'))$

P´ is supported from below: if P were to be smaller than P´, a larger fraction of the bits transmitted would be overhead bits. P´ is supported from above: if P were to be larger than P´, a larger fraction of the bits transmitted would be those of retransmissions of more-likely-to-be damaged packets. This result is intuitively appealing. As per packet overhead (H) goes to zero, so too does the packet size which maximizes effective capacity (P´). As the error rate (E) goes to zero, P´ grows without bound.

Exponential Error Model. If we begin by assuming that the length of errorless bit sequences on the channel are exponentially distributed with mean 1/E bits (i.e., if we again assume a binary symmetric channel), then we get the exponential version of Equation 3-13:

(Eq. 3-16) $$L = 1 - e^{-E*P}$$ $(0 \le E << 1, A << P)$

By substituting our expression for the probability of packet error (L) due to exponentially distributed error interarrival times (Equation 3-16) into our expression for total effective capacity (Equation 3-11) and by maximizing on packet size (P), we get:

(Eq. 3-17) $$P' = \frac{H*B}{2} + \text{SQRT}\left(\frac{H^2*B^2}{4} + \frac{H*B}{E}\right)$$ $(0 \le E << 1)$
$(A << P)$

Note that for relatively low error rates (i.e., H*B*E<<1) this result does agree with that of the linear approximation (Eq. 3-15), as expected.

We have just derived two closed-form expressions giving a packet size which maximizes total effective capacity for feedback correction with two simple error models. These expressions may prove useful as rules of thumb in determining packet size, but more importantly, a general method for considering errors has been demonstrated.

Pareto Error Model. Measurements have shown that a truncated Pareto distribution for "inter-error intervals" is more descriptive of actual telephone circuits than distributions describing a binary symmetric channel <Berger, Sussman>. The truncated Pareto distribution reflects the clustering of errors (i.e., "burst errors") on telephone circuits. The distribution leads to a function for the probability of packet transmission error (L) which has two parameters taking into account, roughly, the mean transmission error rate and the clustering of errors. The first we call X and corresponds to a packet length above which the probability of packet error is assumed to be 1. The second we call Y and corresponds roughly to a measure of error clustering. The probability of retransmission, taken as the probability of packet error as a function of packet length, is given by:

(Eq. 3-18) $L = (P/X)^Y$ ($0 \leq Y \leq 1$, $0 \leq P \leq X$, $A \ll P$)

As with the two previous error models, it is a simple matter to substitute our expression for L into Equation 3-11 to get the dependence of total effective capacity on packet size. With the Pareto model, the closed-form solution for the capacity-maximizing packet size is too complex to be useful here, and we therefore fall back on some numerical comparisons using ARPANET parameters.

The expressions for L in the linear and exponential models have one free parameter, E, the error rate expressed in error bits per transmitted bit. For the ARPANET, E is reported to be on the order of .00001 <Ornstein>. In the Pareto model, the expression for L has two free parameters: X, the maximum length of an error-free packet in bits, and Y, the indicator of error clustering. For our very rough calculations, we take Y from some early measurements of telephone circuits <Berger, Sussman> to be .7 and choose X so that the mean error rate is E, above. (Note that our Y corresponds to Sussman's one minus alpha.)

From Equation 3-18 we derive the truncated Pareto distribution's probability density function and calculate the mean length of an inter-error interval; this mean is equated to 1/E.

(Eq. 3-19) $\dfrac{Y}{Y+1} * X = \dfrac{1}{E}$ ($0 \leq Y \leq 1$)

Substituting .7 for Y and .00001 for E we get an X which fits our distribution to the approximated characteristics of ARPANET 50 Kbps circuits; the maximum length of a error-free packet is taken to be X= 243,000 bits.

It should be understood that the error properties of telephone circuits are very difficult to characterize, due especially to their dependence on length of circuit and time of day <Kahn2, Erank1>. The parameters chosen for our examination are representative of those found in the literature <Berger, Kahn2, Ornstein, Sussman>; they serve mainly to establish the shape of our curves. The formulas are simple enough so that their applicability can be easily judged for many media.

We now plot the theoretical total effective capacity of ARPANET circuits as a function of packet size, using each of our three error models (i.e., Equations 3-13, 3-16, 3-18). Additional parameter values required for the evaluation of Equation 3-11 are B, H, and C as defined immediately before Equation 3-8, above. For the ARPANET, the fixed per bit overhead factor B is 1 (i.e., no per bit overhead). The fixed per packet overhead H (i.e., header) is approximately 136 bits (i.e., 6 8-bit circuit control characters, 24 bits of cyclic checksum provided by hardware, and approximately 4 16-bit words of software control information). The nominal bit rate C is 50,000 bits per second (50 Kbps).

Note that both Equation 3-15 and Equation 3-17 indicate that we can expect total effective capacity to reach its maximum at packet sizes near about 3700 bits. See Figure 3-3.

We have shown how a simple feedback-correction protocol works to provide reliable communication and how bit rate, propagation delay, packet overhead, and transmission errors combine to determine the effective capacity of a channel under the protocol. We have shown that there is an important choice to be made in selecting a packet size and have demonstrated how to calculate the capacity-maximizing packet size for three simple error models.

In an evaluation of our formulas using parameters approximating those of the ARPANET, we have discovered that the total effective capacity of circuits is insensitive to choices of packet size over a wide range. It is interesting that the actual ARPANET packet size of 1000 hits is at the bottom of the acceptable range. We now turn to consider other factors in the design of a store-and-forward packet communications system.

Hop-By-Hop versus End-By-End Acknowledging

Let D be some large distance between a primary sender and a primary receiver, where D is expressed in the number of seconds required for a bit to propagate between the sender and receiver through an uninterrupted circuit. D is so large that we are to consider placing some number of intermediate, store-and-forward, feedback-correction nodes between the primary sender and receiver. Let d, as before, be the distance between intermediate nodes so that the number of circuit hops used is D/d.

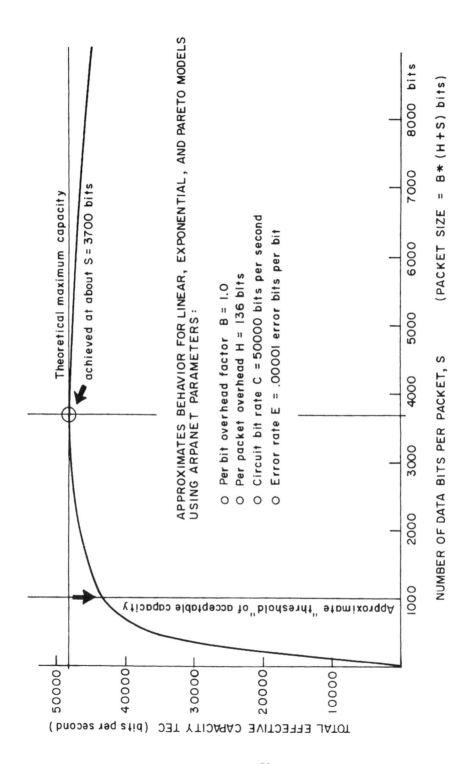

FIGURE 3-3 TOTAL EFFECTIVE CAPACITY VERSUS PACKET SIZE

50

A packet originating at the primary sender (i.e., the source node) will need to travel over D/d circuit hops passing through (D/d)-1 intermediate store-and-forward nodes before arriving at the primary receiver (i.e., the destination node).

The question is whether it would be better to propagate a packet by acknowledging its successful transfer hop-by-hop or end-by-end: should intermediate store-and-forward nodes use a feedback-correction protocol across each circuit hop or should they simply forward packets for end-to-end feedback correction?

Using Equation 3-7 with T=((2d)+(A/C)), we get that the mean time for an acknowledged one-hop packet transfer is ((P/C)+2d+(A/C))/(1-L) seconds. There are D/d hops so that the mean time for a successful end-to-end hop-by-hop acknowledged packet transfer is:

$$\text{(Eq. 3-20)} \qquad \text{Mean Time} = \frac{(D/d) * ((P/C) + 2d + (A/C))}{(1 - L)} \qquad (0 \le L < 1)$$

The time required for a packet-ACK end-to-end round trip is (D/d)*((P/C)+2d+(A/C)) seconds. Assuming, as before, that La<<Lp and that the probability of a successful end-to-end packet transfer is 1-L to the D/d power, and therefore that L=Lp, the mean time for a successful end-by-end acknowledged packet transfer is:

$$\text{(Eq. 3-21)} \qquad \text{Mean Time} = \frac{(D/d) * ((P/C) + 2d + (A/C))}{(1 - L)^{(D/d)}} \qquad (0 \le L < 1)$$

Comparing Equations 20 and 21, we see that hop-by-hop acknowledging is superior to end-by-end acknowledging; (l-L)**(D/d) is generally smaller than (1-L). Hop-by-hop acknowledging is the obvious choice when the retransmission probability L is large or when many hops are required with any non-negligible L.

The ARPANET uses hop-by-hop acknowledging. Taking .00001 as the probability of an ARPANET circuit bit error <Ornstein> and 1000 as the number of bits per packet, we arrive at a pessimistic value for L (ignoring error clustering) of 1%. If we also make the rather pessimistic assumption that a packet typically makes 10 hops from source to destination (the number is closer to 5), then Equations 20 and 21 tell us that the use of hop-by-hop acknowledging buys only a 9% reduction of mean end-to-end transfer time. Measurements have been made which do show that, on a 1000 mile 50 Kbps circuit, L can go as high as .1 for long periods <Frank1>. Taking this L and the pessimistic 10-hop assumption, we calculate from Equations 20 and 21 that the use of hop-by-hop acknowledging buys a 57% reduction of mean end-to-end transfer time. Experience with the ARPANET has shown that, when a circuit is working at all, its error rates put L well below 1% and make our 9% an upper bound on the savings due to hop-by-hop acknowledging.

Consider what using end-by-end acknowledging might mean to our use of memory in a store-and-forward network. Because intermediate nodes would not have to store packets after forwarding, their memory requirements might be reduced. Because the primary senders would have to store pending packets for at least one roundtrip time through the network, their memory requirements might be increased. It can be strongly argued that memory at the "ends" of a network, in its HOSTs, is much cheaper than that scattered among its switching nodes. Similarly, it can be argued that retransmission in the special-purpose switching nodes of a network, in its IMPs, is much cheaper than that which can be provided in its general-purpose HOSTs. A question remains.

Another question which this analysis raises is whether the complication brought to the store-and-forward subnet with hop-by-hop acknowledging is justified by the resulting performance improvement. As indicated, this question is hard to answer for the ARPANET, especially without the relevant data, but one could imagine networks in which the choice between hop-by-hop and end-by-end acknowledging is clearer; we note that work done, quite independently, by the Network Analysis Corporation raises similar question for the ARPA Packet Radio Network to be discussed in the next chapter <NAC1>.

Store-and-Forward Node Spacing

It has been found that the error properties of ARPANET telephone circuits vary with circuit length. Long-haul circuits have measureably higher error rates than do short-haul circuits <Frank1, Kahn2>. We ask the general question of whether there exists some spacing of store-and-forward feedback-correction nodes which optimizes the flow of packets over noisy communication paths. For a simple distance-dependent exponential error model, we show that an optimal inter-node distance does exist. Applying our result to the ARPANET, we find that factors other than circuit error properties (e.g., cost, delay) must dominate in IMP placement.

Assuming the use of a hop-by-hop acknowledgment scheme in a presumably error prone and/or very large store-and-forward network, we have Equation 3-20 for mean packet transfer time, where L is the probability of a packet error in one hop. For reasons of tractability, we adopt a simple exponential error model involving a constant per hop term U and a distance dependent term d*F:

(Eq. 3-22)
$$L = 1 - e^{-(U + (d*F))}$$

U and F might be functions of, say, packet size and time of day <Frank1>; d is taken to be the distance in seconds between store-and-forward nodes. Substituting for L in Equation 3-20 according to Equation 3-22, differentiating with respect to d, setting equal to zero, and solving for d (all using MACSYMA via the ARPANET <Metcalfe8, Wang>), we get an expression for the internode distance (in seconds) which minimizes the mean transfer time across an arbitrary number of store-and-forward nodes:

(Eq. 3-23)
$$d' = SQRT\left(\frac{P}{2C*F}\right)$$
$$(A \ll P)$$
$$((F*(P/C)) \ll 1)$$

Using very crude data on the performance of ARPANET 50 Kbps circuits <Frank1>, we obtain a fit to the exponential error model in Equation 3-22 with a U of .033 and an F of .004. While believing the data to be inaccurate (on the pessimistic side <Ornstein>) and the model to be overly simplistic, we evaluate Equation 3-23 for the ARPANET to discover that the inter-node distance which minimizes the effect of transmission errors on transmission delay is almost 300,000 miles. This result supports the belief that distance-dependent error properties of ARPA circuits can be neglected and leads us to agree that other factors must be dominant in IMP placement <Frank 1>. One could imagine networks in which this (or perhaps some more exact) formulation would be useful.

Store-and-Forward Delay and Packet Size

It is important in communications among interactive computers (e.g., in the ARPANET) that transmission delay be low. The maximization of effective capacity does not always lead to a minimization of transfer delay. Choices of packet size in a store-and-forward network, in particular, trade-off effective capacity against delay.

In a raw circuit, propagation delay and bit rate are independent; delay is a function of circuit length, and bit rate is a function of transmission bandwidth. When a store-and-forward node interrupts a circuit between a sender and receiver, the transmission of bits from sender to receiver is then subject to a packet time's worth of delay, P/C seconds, which we term "store-and-forward delay". Store-and-forward delay is caused by a node's requirement that it completely receive and store a packet before forwarding it. Note that store-and-forward delay is introduced even when a node's packet handling time (e.g., for error checking and routing) is zero.

When packet size approaches one bit, store-and-forward delay becomes negligible, approaching one bit time. When packet size grows very large, store-and-forward delay grows linearly with it. Because packet time (P/C) is related inversely to the raw channel's bit rate, we say that a store-and-forward node converts limited capacity (i.e., bit rate) into delay.

As seen in Equation 3-20, if there is more than one store-and-forward node between a sender and receiver, then each of them contributes at least a packet time's delay, P/C seconds, to the total packet transfer time.

As packet length increases from zero, the effective capacity and delay increase together. In this region of low packet size, we buy increases in effective capacity with increases in delay. The more delay we are willing to tolerate, the higher the effective capacity available. After a certain point (e.g., that given in Equation 3-15), increases in packet length increase delay and decrease effective capacity.

In an interactive network, the requirement of low delay restricts the length of packets carrying interactive traffic. In the ARPANET, the packet size of 1000 bits is at the low end of the range of packet sizes which produce acceptable effective capacity (see Figure 3-3).

As an aside, we note that the interdependence of capacity and delay is fundamental to packet communication. Here, we find that intermediate store-and-forward packet-switching nodes convert limited capacity into delay; in Appendices A and B we find that the flow control required in networks of computers converts delay into limited capacity.

Message Disassembly

Based on the preceding, it is reasonable to expect that packet communications systems of different characteristics and applications will require different packet sizes. We ask whether it is also reasonable to expect data passing across an interface between different systems to be repackaged, i.e., to be repacketed, so that their passage through both systems will be efficient. With message disassembly in the ARPANET as an example and with tools developed in preceding sections, we briefly develop some of the issues in impedance matching at communications system interfaces.

As discussed earlier, ARPANET HOSTs deal with up to 8095 bit messages across their error-free, 100 Kbps IMP-HOST interfaces. These messages are disassembled producing up to 8 packets of about 1000 bits each, by the IMPs, for transmission over noisy, 50 Kbps telephone circuits. Packets of a single HOST message are reassembled at their destination IMP for transmission out of the IMP system into the destination HOST.

We find it useful to view the IMP Subnet as one packet communication system comprising IMPs and telephone circuits, and each of the HOSTs as another packet communication system comprising processes and HOST-specific communication paths. The IMP-HOST hardware interface, with associated IMP-HOST protocol at each end, is yet another packet communication system with parameters all its own. The introduction of Satellite IMPs into the ARPANET with their very long delay "circuits" (250 milliseconds) <Abramson4> constitutes yet another packet communication system.

We now ask why the IMPs do message disassembly. Why disassemble an 8095 bit HOST message into 8 IMP packets of about 1000 bits each?

Store-and-forward delay. The most compelling reason for disassembly in the ARPANET is the dependence of store-and-forward delay on packet size. A P=8000 bit packet, moving over C=50 Kbps circuit, would be delayed a minimum of (P/C)=.16 seconds per store-and-forward node. A packet going cross-country through the ARPANET will typically encounter more than 5 IMPs, giving a minimum cross-country transit delay for an 8000 bit packet of about .8 seconds. Even this minimum transit delay would exceed that required for console interaction across the country <Roberts>. And this minimum transit delay would not take into account (1) the time required for packet queuing inside

IMPs, (2) the effect of retransmission, or (3) the likelihood of l0-hop transit times.

A 1000 bit packet is delayed a minimum of .02 seconds per IMP, giving a minimum cross-country transit delay (for 5 IMPs again) of .1 second. With the 1000 bit packets, the .5 second cross-country transit time specification <Roberts> is met; actual measurements put the typical transit time under .2 seconds <Frank1>.

Looking at Figure 3-3, we see that 8000 bit packets are well beyond the size which maximizes theoretical total effective capacity (i.e., 3700 bits) and that 1000 bit packets support less than, but only slightly less than, maximum total effective capacity.

Therefore, one concludes, message disassembly is essential for supporting interactive communication.

This conclusion ignores the fact, as does our preceding analysis, that the ARPANET's interactive traffic is characterized by packets of well under 1000 bits. The proposition that interactive traffic should encounter low delays and that sustained volume traffic can tolerate higher delays may undermine reasoning for ARPANET message disassembly <McQuillan>. Having a 4000 bit maximum size for packets, say, and no disassembly, would improve the throughput characteristics of volume traffic while only slightly increasing the delay of interactive traffic.

Parallel packet propagation. There are multiple paths between nodes in the ARPANET. Disassembly makes it possible for an 8000 bit message to use these multiple paths in parallel. Packets from a single message can propagate through different paths. The effective capacity of the ARPANET between various nodes often exceeds that over any one circuit.

If HOSTs were willing to assume more responsibility for their communications, however, they could use 4000 bit (or 1000 bit) messages and their own sequencing schemes to derive any benefits from parallel packet propagation.

Fixed-length buffer allocation. For reasons of speed and efficiency, the IMPs maintain fixed length packet buffers. Because HOST messages may vary in size between 32 and 8095 bits, a packet size of 8095 bits would require a fixed buffer size of 8095 bits. A high frequency of small packets would result in very poor utilization of IMP storage. Assuming that HOST message sizes are uniformly distributed between 1 and $N=8095$ bits and assuming that a packet header is of fixed length $H=136$ bits, then, it can be shown <Frank1> that the fixed packet buffer size which makes best use of IMP memory is about $P'=1000$ bits, according to:

$$\text{(Eq. 3—24)} \qquad\qquad P' = SQRT\ (H*N)$$

The distribution of HOST message sizes is not known, especially since ARPANET use has been low and limited artificially to interactive traffic. Neither is it known whether 8095 bits is a suitable message size for HOSTs <Roberts>. Still, IMP buffer storage is scarce and its utilization is an important consideration; but then 1000-bit (and not 4000-bit) message-packets might be preferred.

Packet size and queueing delay. It is tempting to suggest that the IMP packet size be larger than 1000 bits (say 4000 bits) to improve effective capacity and to eliminate disassembly by reducing maximum HOST message size to that of an IMP packet. The rationale might be that small packets typical of interactive traffic will experience small store-and-forward delays and that large packets will experience large store-and-forward delays, by virtue of their size (P/C). However, the queueing of packets in IMPs results in long packets interfering with short ones. Even if short packets were given priority in modem queues, a short packet would still have to wait for a long packet already in transmission. A scheme whereby short packets pre-empt long packets might promise to eliminate even completion delays, but then the effective capacity of circuits would be reduced by the presence of pre-empted, incomplete, and therefore discarded long packets.

Reassembly lock-up and IMP buffer allocation. The most compelling arguments against IMP message disassembly relate to the additional complexity required in the IMP program to deal with difficulties of message reassembly. The most famous bug in the initial implementation of the IMP Subnet is the "reassembly lock-up problem" <Frank1, McQuillan>.

The deadlock-prone activity of collecting undiscardable packets in a finite pool of buffers for reassembly has been reorganized in more recent versions of the IMP program <McQuillan>.

The general strategy adopted in recent versions of the IMP calls for the pre-allocation of 8 buffers in a destination IMP for a multi-packet message. When a multi-packet message begins to arrive at an IMP from one of its HOSTs, the IMP-HOST interface involved is hung until it can be confirmed that 8 buffers have been allocated at the destination IMP. The confirmation is obtained via a control packet exchange between the source and destination IMPs. If two multi-packet messages between the same pair of IMPs follow closely enough together, the allocation confirmation is skipped because the destination IMP automatically reallocates the same 8 buffers to the same source IMP for a certain short period of time. This strategy may indeed prevent reassembly lock-up as claimed, but at a cost.

While a multi-packet message waits for its buffer allocation to be confirmed, the IMP-HOST interface at the sending HOST is blocked and all outgoing traffic (including interactive traffic) is delayed accordingly. While a multi-packet message is winding its way through the IMP Subnet, 8 packet buffers sit idle at the destination IMP.

It is premature to conclude that the new strategy used to make message reassembly work is less effective than a strategy without message disassembly at all; as IMPs and circuits become faster and store-and-forward delay lower, the conclusion will become more attractive.

Distance Independence

The ARPANET is built so that, to its users, distance doesn't matter. Accounting is performed on the number of packets transmitted by a HOST, independent of destination, and, as we have just seen, basic parameters of the communications subnet are derived from the principle that even the most distant interactions should experience negligible delay. After all, the very purpose of communication is to make distance less of an obstacle. But, from what we've learned, distance-independence as an inviolate principle has serious implications on design.

To make the distance-dependent component of delay negligibly small in a store-and-forward network, throughput, or what we call "capacity", must be sacrificed and, to minimize this sacrifice, the complexity of the subnet significantly increased; evidence, message disassembly.

A certain greater degree of distance-dependence seems inescapable. Packets winding their way from one end to another of a national utility network will, in their travels from IMP to IMP, use much more of the network's resources than packets going only a hop or two. It will prove economically unsound to bill out the aggregate use of processor cycles, buffer seconds, and baud miles on a simple per-packet basis when the use of these resources is so directly dependent on packet miles.

Although this is not the place to extol the virtues of marginal-cost pricing, we must quickly point out that an anomalous distance-dependence, in the form of seconds delay (rather than dollars), has already started the ARPANET toward more economical use of its resources. The University of Hawaii is 250 milliseconds from its nearest neighbor on the ARPANET (via satellite) which puts it well over a half second from its most distant neighbors. The delay between Hawaii and California is still down in the range where the use of interactive computers through the ARPANET's TELNET is tolerable; the delay to Boston computers, however, is just large enough to make TELNET use intolerable. Hawaii is working (with others) to design and build a TELNET-like system which does a better job of managing echoing so as to minimize the effects of transmission delay on conversational computing; this system, at the same time, promises to reduce the amount of packet traffic necessary to support a computer terminal user <Davidson>.

Distance-independence is more a characteristic of broadcast communication; if, for example, we can send a packet up to a satellite repeater, then the cost of delivering that packet back down to a ground station is independent of where that station is over a range of many thousands of miles.

We now turn our attention, in the following two chapters, to the organization of communication systems based on broadcast media. We find that broadcast systems complement point-to-point systems in at least two important ways: broadcast networks provide us with more economical organizations of very long distance transmission, using satellite radio, and of very short distance mobile transmission, using ground radio.

Packet Radio Networks

Radio is a broadcast medium; a radio transmitter generates signals which can be detected over a wide area by any number of radio receivers. As one might expect, the application of packet communication techniques to radio has led to novel system organizations of a kind different from those of point-to-point transmission media. Indeed, packet communication opens up a spectrum of broadcast system organizations.

Summary

In this chapter we briefly described three related packet radio systems: one that works, one being built, and one being planned. The purpose of our description is to summarize a recent history of developments in packet radio and to motivate interest in solutions to packet radio problems. In the next chapter, we move from this description to theories about system behavior.

The ALOHA Network is a terminal-computer packet radio system in operation at the University of Hawaii. Many so-called "ALOHA techniques" in packet communication have come from the experience of Hawaii's historically important packet radio network <Abramson, Kuo>.

The ARPANET Satellite System will soon expand the ARPANET's store-and-forward IMP system to include the utilization of the broadcast capabilities of earth-orbiting satellite radio repeaters. Work on the satellite system has contributed significantly to the development of so-called "advanced ALOHA techniques" in packet communication <Abramson6, Binder1, Crowther, Metcalfe9, Roberts3, Roberts4>.

The ARPA Packet Radio Network is based on hand-held personal terminals whose communications evolved from the ALOHA concept; planning is now in progress toward building a prototype system <NAC, Roberts2>. The very large numbers of inexpensive and highly mobile terminals envisioned for such a system offer an advance in our ability to deliver computing.

The ALOHA Network

The ALOHA Network <Abramson, Abramson1, Suo> is a packet radio terminal-computer communications system in operation at the University of Hawaii. The ALOHA Network is important in that aspects of its design will find applications in the utilization of satellite links, cable TV, multi-drop broadcast cable <Mason>, and other communications media.

The ALOHA System has been assigned two 100 KHz radio channels in the UHF band, each of which now operates at 24 kilobits per second (Kbps). The channels are used for communication between an IBM 360/65 and a number of terminals scattered among the Hawaiian Islands. A communications computer (a HP 2115A) at the 360/65 receives data packets from the population of terminals over one UHF channel; it transmits acknowledgments and data packets back out to those terminals over the second UHF channel. Each of the terminals is equipped with a UHF transceiver and assorted logic for (1) preparing terminal-input packets for radio transmission, (2) receiving acknowledgments of successful packet transmission, (3) retransmitting data packets if need be, and (4) receiving data for presentation as terminal output (see Figure 4-1).

The transmission of data from the central computer facility outward to the computer terminals is a relatively simple first-come first-served, sequential process. Messages marked for transmission are queued by the central computer and are transmitted one after the other. Each terminal receives all transmissions, but is constructed so as to discard messages not addressed to it. Outward going messages require retransmission infrequently, only when they are damaged by random noise in the radio channel.

The coordination of the transmissions of data from the widely distributed terminals in toward the central facility is the "random-access" or broadcast communications problem. The traditional solutions to this problem call for some sort of "orthogonal" multiplexing technique (i.e., in time or frequency) whereby each terminal is assigned a dedicated slice of the channel going from it to the central facility. When transmitting, a terminal is limited according to that frac-

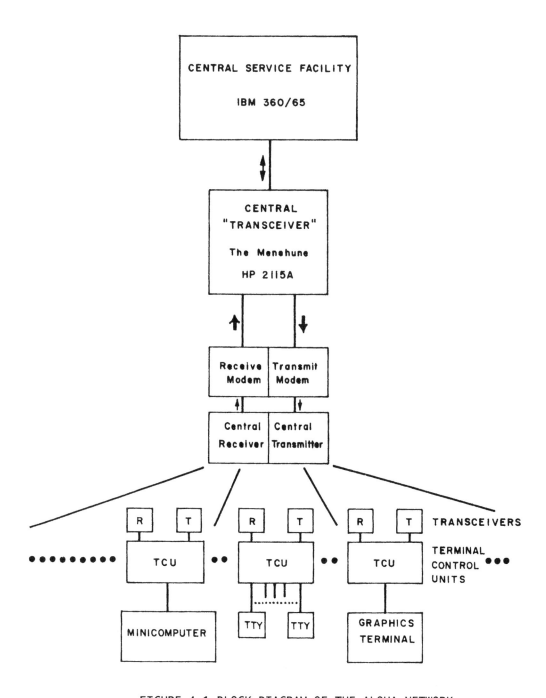

FIGURE 4-1 BLOCK DIAGRAM OF THE ALOHA NETWORK

tion of the channel assigned to it, and, when not transmitting, a terminal wastes that fraction. Thus, in cases where the peak bandwidth requirement of a terminal is large relative to the mean, either the terminal's performance is significantly reduced by its small share of the channel or a large fraction of the channel is wasted between terminal bursts.

The multiplexing scheme adopted for the ALOHA system is intended to overcome the deficiencies of orthogonal multiplexing under burst usage. The original unembellished ALOHA multiplexing scheme is a kind of "asynchronous time-division multiplexing" (ATDM) <Chu, Pack> which we call the "classical ALOHA system". The ALOHA or "random access" system compares favorably with other ATDM systems, namely the Polling and Loop systems <Hayes>.

Under the ALOHA system, terminals prepare input data packets and transmit them at will for reception by the central station. A given data packet may fail to arrive safely at the central station due to transmission errors caused (1) by random noise errors and/or (2) by interference with packets transmitted simultaneously from other terminals. A 32 bit cyclic checksum is used by the central facility to detect transmission errors of either kind so that damaged packets can be discarded. If a terminal fails to receive an acknowledgment for a pending data packet within some time-out period, the terminal retransmits the packet to try again for successful transmission. Note that the retransmission time-out period must be different from terminal to terminal or time to time so that interfering transmissions will not repeat their collisions ad infinitum. The ALOHA Network uses randomized retransmission intervals <Hayes>.

Under the classical ALOHA system, terminal transmissions are completely unsynchronized and occupy no fixed portion of the channel. When a terminal requires a burst of the channel during its peak activity, it takes it, at the risk of some small delay due to packet collision and retransmission. When a terminal is idle, it uses none of the channel, leaving the full channel bandwidth for other terminals. The extent to which this ALOHA scheme is effective goes directly with the "burstiness" of terminal transmissions. As the ALOHA channel gets full, i.e., as the mean aggregate bit-rate reaches 1/2 channel capacity, interference among packets in the ALOHA channel causes total throughput to approach its maximum value of 18% channel capacity <Abramson, Abramson1>. In various studies of the ALOHA system, detailed models have led to more accurate analyses of performance and to practical techniques for improving the behavior of ALOHA-based systems.

Slotting. A simple technique, slotting, leads to a system known as "slotted ALOHA" wherein packet transmissions are made to fall into slots defined by the ticking of some global clock. Under such a scheme, packets still collide, but less often due to the fact that slotting tends to isolate packets across slot boundaries. Slotting has the effect of doubling the maximum possible throughput of an ALOHA channel <Roberts3>. Slotting is achieved simply by having terminals hold off the start of packet transmission until the end of a packet from the central transmitter. The problem of getting effective slot synchronization grows with the range of the transceivers involved, i.e., with the propagation delays which can lead to slots much larger than the packets they contain.

Single Frequency. Considerations of frequency conservation and terminal simplicity have generated interest in single-frequency ALOHA systems. In such a system, packets to and from the central receiver are interleaved or, possibly, the central receiver disappears yielding a terminal-terminal communication system. In the case of multiple central receivers, the single frequency system has the advantage that a mobile terminal can wander in and out of the range of various transceivers without changing its transmission frequency and possibly benefitting from multiple paths to its destination <NAC>.

Capture. A feature of radio receivers is that they can get multiple transmissions at their antenna and still capture only one if its power is sufficiently stronger than those of the interfering transmissions. This capture effect can benefit the performance of an ALOHA system in that packet collisions need not be fatal to all of the packets concerned. The capture effect has been studied in trying to determine to what extent modulation techniques which exhibit "good capture" should be favored over modulation techniques with, for example, high bit rates or long range <Roberts3>.

Carrier Sense. If a terminal could determine whether some other terminal (presumably farther from the central receiver) has committed to send a packet in the very next slot, then that terminal could abstain from transmitting so as to avoid collision. Such a determination would help everyone. It turns out that a radio receiver can detect the presence of a transmission within a few bits and therefore it appears possible to use this "carrier sense" technique to further reduce the collision rate in an ALOHA channel <Abramson6>. We notice that carrier sense techniques give priority to distant terminals while making everyone better off; carrier sense might also be used to compensate for the priority given nearer terminals by the capture effect.

Retransmission Control. When two or more packets collide in an ALOHA channel, the terminals involved must determine when to retransmit. The retransmission interval must be randomly determined to avoid repeated packet collisions ad infinitum. As studied in the following chapter, the choice of a retransmission mechanism is critical in determining the performance of the ALOHA channel under varying load. It has been shown that performance under light loads trades off against performance under heavy loads in a system with a simple, fixed retransmission interval generator. By controlling the retransmission interval generator as a function of channel utilization, an ALOHA system can be made to perform well over a wide range of system loads (even into saturation) <Metcalfe9>.

The ARPANET Satellite System

With recent growth of the ARPANET has come an interest in earth-orbiting satellite radio repeaters for economy of long-range digital communication, especially for crossing the Pacific and Atlantic Oceans. It is already a routine matter to acquire a "voice circuit" from Hawaii to California which, while behaving like a normal telephone circuit in all other ways, is provided via COMSAT satellite and imposes a propagation delay on the order of 250 milliseconds <Abramson4>. However, a satellite radio repeater is a broadcast device whose potential is far from realized in a point-to-point mode of operation. The satellite link between Hawaii and California could be used by any number of ground stations in China, Japan, Alaska, Hawaii, California and moving points in the Pacific <Abramson3, Abramson4, Abramson5, Abramson7>.

Toward making full use of broadcast satellite communications, ARPA is well into a project to build satellite IMPs (SIMPs) for the ARPANET, using communication techniques derived from those of the ALOHA system <Binder1, Crowther, Roberts4>. Considerable progress has been made in developing and analyzing ALOHA-based schemes for multiple ground station coordination of broadcast satellite communication (see Figure 4-2) <Kleinrock3>.

The ALOHA techniques being studied for application by satellite ground stations depart from the "classical ALOHA system" because (1) there is no central receiver to coordinate terminal behavior, (2) all ground stations transmit on one frequency and receive on another, (3) the delay from packet transmission to packet receipt is on the order of many packet times rather than negligibly small fractions of a packet time, (4) the number of ground stations (corresponding to terminals in the classical ALOHA system) is to be in the tens rather than hun-

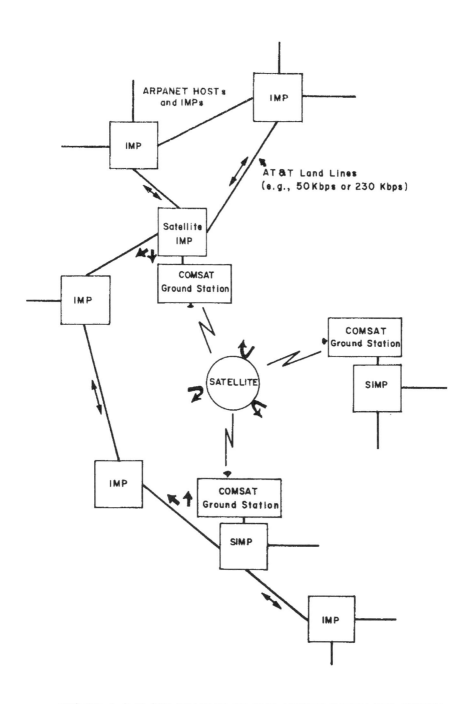

FIGURE 4-2 BLOCK DIAGRAM OF THE ARPNET SATELLITE SYSTEM

dreds or thousands, and (5) each of the ground stations will generate traffic for the satellite system at a rate considerably more uniform than that of a terminal with a single human user.

At present, there are at least three proposals being considered for use by SIMPs. It is likely that many more such proposals will be generated before implementation begins and that the scheme chosen will draw on many of those offered. The three current proposals emphasize the need to reduce the number of packet collisions in the satellite channel as channel traffic becomes heavy and therefore more uniform on a per-ground-station basis.

Reservation-ALOHA. The Reservation-ALOHA scheme proposed by the future implementers of the SIMP at BBN, introduces the notion of a "frame" containing a satellite round-trip time's worth of packet slots. Any given ground station determines the "reservation" of slots in the current frame based on observations of the previous frame. Slots which a particular ground station successfully used in the previous frame are reserved for it to use again. Slots used by other ground stations in the previous frame are off limits. Slots in which no successful transmissions occurred in the previous frame are up for grabs, are ALOHA slots. The Reservation-ALOHA scheme promises nearly full channel utilization under heavy loads and is simple. The scheme does very well with the component of constant traffic from any given ground station while suffering somewhat under varying, bursty loads <Crowther>.

Interleaved Reservation-ALOHA. The Interleaved Reservation-ALOHA scheme, proposed by Roberts of ARPA, introduces a controlled partitioning of the satellite channel into an ALOHA portion and a reservation portion. As a ground station accumulates packets due to arrivals, collisions, and random noise, it announces through the channel its requirement for a reservation of an appropriate number of slots (up to a limit) and, based on a knowledge of previous announcements by other ground stations, it determines unambiguously which future slots are thereby reserved for its transmissions. As traffic increases, the fraction of ALOHA slots decreases allowing nearly full channel utilization. Because reservations are blocked, overhead due to a ground station's need to turn its transmitter on and off can be amortized over a number of packets. The scheme is only slightly more complex than the Reservation-ALOHA scheme in that it requires ground stations to keep an accounting of reservations across many slots and to maintain the dynamically changing partition between ALOHA and reserved slots <Roberts4>.

Priority Reservation-ALOHA. The most recent scheme for coordinating satellite ground stations, from Binder at the University of Hawaii, adds a priority scheme to the frame mechanism so that slot conflicts can be resolved within two frame times, requiring at most one retransmission per packet. Some slots are said to be owned and a slot's owner is guaranteed access within two frames by requiring that conflicts in an owned slot be resolved in the next frame by requiring non-owning ground stations to desist.

Beyond ownership, slots are assigned, as in the Reservation-ALOHA system, according to recent traffic levels, but with a globally known priority. The priority assignment permits ground stations to straightforwardly resolve conflicts in one frame for the next frame. This ownership-priority scheme requires considerably more bookkeeping than either of the previous schemes. We await analysis of its performance <Binder1>.

The Hand-Held Personal Terminal

At the 1972 SJCC, Roberts proposed a design for a hand-held personal terminal which combined recent advances of our understanding of ALOHA packet communication and electronics miniaturization to deliver a long-awaited and slightly updated Dick Tracy wrist radio. Since then, ARPA has organized a packet radio project to advance that design toward an operational system. While it is difficult to estimate the impact of such an advance in computer communication, we believe that of all the packet radio networks, this has the highest potential for revolutionizing both communication and computing <Roberts2>.

Applications. Current thinking on the subject places a wide variety of "terminals" (possibly) moving through grids of radio repeater transceivers spread around the world. One such terminal might be a wrist-mounted computer-transceiver offering a wide variety of inquiry and communication services to its wandering owner; another terminal might be a weather or seismic monitor parachuted into a dense forest; yet another might be a hand-held voice transceiver like a walkie-talkie; another might be an onboard air traffic control computer exchanging packets with an FAA control center about its position; still another might be a lap-held computer used by children in their homes as a super-toy <Papert>, able to access lesson materials, libraries, and teachers as desired; and so on.

Design Considerations. Little is known about how to organize such a packet radio system. So far only the broadest of system organization questions have been considered <NAC>.

Transceiver Size and Range. Careful consideration must be given to the trade-offs on transceiver size and range. Pocket-held, hand-held, lap-held, table-held, and truck-held packet radio terminals each will place different constraints on transceiver range and therefore on grid spacing. The variance in terminal characteristics may be such as to require multiple, overlapping packet radio systems based on area cover and application, but the hope is, as in the case of the ARPANET, that a fairly general purpose network can be built to fill needs over a wide range. There are, of course, many economies in having multiple applications share the same packet communications facilities.

Stations. In moving toward a design for such a general purpose system, thought must be given to the placement of packet radio stations (corresponding roughly to the central receiver in the classical ALOHA system). Stations will control the interfacing of the packet radio terminal system to service facilities. Such facilities might include systems for private terminal-terminal communication, for data base inquiry and updating, for direct access to general purpose computing systems, or, as envisioned for the ARPA prototype, for interconnection with another communication system like the ARPANET.

Repeaters. Stations will need to be sized according to the anticipated terminal population to be serviced. Due to variations in population density, the geographical area to be serviced by a station will vary. To compensate for such traffic density induced range variations, something called a "packet radio repeater" may be required in relatively sparse areas. The need for such repeaters adds a new kind of complexity to considerations of system organization <Frank2, NAC1>.

Single Frequency. For transceiver simplicity, mobility, multipath reliability, and frequency utilization, it seems desirable to have a single frequency system. A single frequency transceiver could move freely amidst a repeater grid, constantly in the range of several repeaters or stations. Neighboring stations, which might otherwise offer disjoint service to an area on different frequencies, could cooperate to pool their traffic in utilization of the same frequency while improving reliability through redundancy.

Routing and Multipath. With multiple repeaters and stations, the routing of packets to their intended destinations becomes non-trivial. That packets may reach a destination by several paths makes it necessary to provide for duplicate suppression. With a forest of repeaters with overlapping ranges, it becomes necessary to prevent unstable regenerative packet duplication (see Figure 4-3).

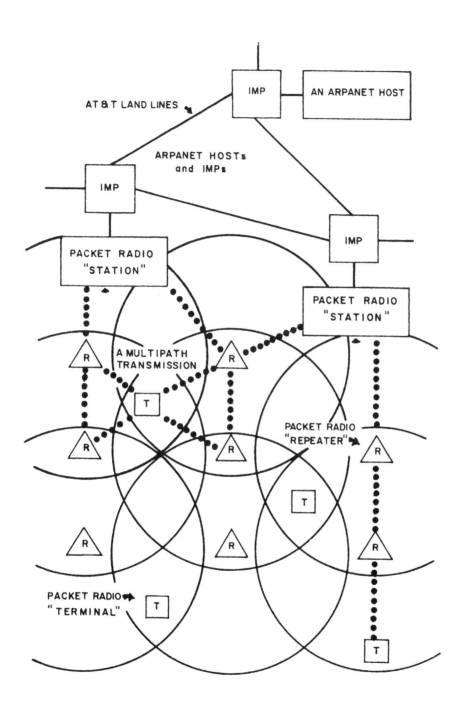

FIGURE 4-3 SPECULATED LAYOUT OF THE ARPA PACKET RADIO NETWORK

Conclusion

The general impact of computers on communication (as embodied in what we call packet communication) is the introduction of a high degree of variability. This impact is clearly seen in the manner in which ALOHA techniques have reduced the synchronization required to make multiplexing systems work. Now that low-synchrony communication is possible, many communication applications which are basically asynchronous can be better supported. As suggested in the preceding survey of packet radio networks, a synchrony spectrum in channel multiplexing is now available (see Figure 4-4).

This breakthrough in our organization of communications need not be restricted to radio, nor even to broadcast media. In the past, broadcast media have been used for point-to-point communication with considerable success, e.g., COMSAT voice channels. It is not too far-fetched to suggest that, for certain applications, point-to-point media might be effectively used under an essentially broadcast organization (see Figure 4-5) <Mason>.

In the next chapter, we turn to detailed analysis of techniques coming directly from the "classical ALOHA system". These techniques promise to find broad application in broadcast packet communication.

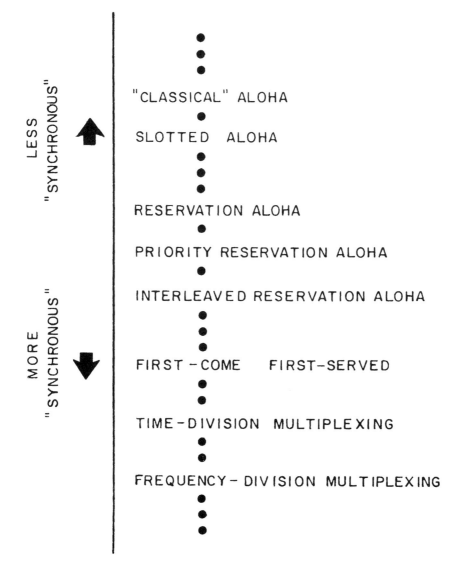

FIGURE 4-4 SYNCHRONY SPECTRUM OF MULTIPLEXING TECHNIQUES

POINT-TO-POINT MEDIA	BROADCAST MEDIA	
PUBLIC TELEPHONE LASER MICROWAVE	AUTOMOBILE RADIO COMSAT SATELLITE VOICE CIRCUITS MICROWAVE	POINT-TO-POINT ORGANIZATION
CABLE TELEVISION IRVINE LOOP NET ALOHA MULTI-DROP CABLE	COMMERCIAL RADIO AND TELEVISION ARPANET SATELLITE SYSTEM ALOHA PACKET RADIO	BROADCAST ORGANIZATION

FIGURE 4-5 BROADCAST / POINT-TO-POINT MEDIA / ORGANIZATION

Analysis of Broadcast Packet Communication

The following analysis begins with a careful reconsideration of Abramson's early model of the classical ALOHA system <Abramson> and leads to the discovery of the importance of ALOHA retransmission control in maintaining stable performance under varying system load. The analysis is intended to apply to broadcast communication systems in general, not only to ALOHA packet radio. The presentation is somewhat descriptive of the history of our thinking about ALOHA systems and attempts to retell the sorting out of issues and refinement of analysis.

With his first, simple model of the "classical ALOHA system", Abramson derived the "ALOHA Result" linking channel throughput and traffic; his analysis, reproduced in the first part of this chapter, assumes Poisson packet arrivals and omits the details of randomized retransmission <Abramson1>. Our reconsideration of Abramson's model, in the second part of this chapter, (1) introduces a finite-source model of packet arrivals to better account for the behavior of interactive terminal users in a loaded system, (2) considers the effect of exponentially distributing retransmission intervals, and (3) extends the analysis to obtain the distribution of user block times (i.e., transmission delays), particularly the mean and variance.

In recent work by Hayes and Sherman, the delay characteristics of the ALOHA system are compared with those of two other ATDN techniques, namely the Polling and Loop systems <Hayes>. But, again, they model packet arrivals with a Poisson process; the same is true of Pack's consideration of ATDM using general results from his analysis of an M/D/1 queueing system <Pack>.

Roberts discovered that a "slotted" ALOHA channel could support twice the throughput of an unslotted channel < Roberts3>; in the latter half of this chapter we develop a discrete-time model of a slotted ALOHA system, once again bringing into account user blocking and randomized retransmission, deriving the block time mean and variance, and then, additionally, discovering "retransmission control" as a technique for achieving acceptable performance and stability over a wide range of system loads, even well into saturation <Metcalfe9>. Where our analysis considers exponentially and geometrically distributed retransmission intervals, Binder, in subsequent analysis, derives results for the uniform distribution <Binder>. Where our analysis studies an ALOHA system in steady state, very recent work by Lu uses first order homogeneous linear difference equations to get a dynamic description of ALOHA system state <Lu>.

The ALOHA Result Revisited

We present a sketch of Abramson's analysis <Abramson, Abramson1> of the ALOHA ATDM multiplexing scheme described in the previous chapter.

Assume the packets sent by terminals are all P bits in length and let the nominal bit-rate of the radio channel be C bits per second. The duration of a packet on the channel is therefore P/C seconds (Abramson's "tau"). Each of the N active users generates new packets of data independently at Poisson rate 1/T packets per second (Abramson's "lambda"). The channel sees an aggregate, new packet arrival process with Poisson rate N/T packets per second. Each packet requires P/C channel seconds; therefore, we compute the channel throughput, analogous to the utilization (rho) of the Erlang queuing model <Drake, Saaty>, as (N*P)/(C*T) channel seconds per second. The total number of packets being transmitted per second is some unknown channel traffic, R. R is greater than N/T because each packet gives rise to some uncertain number of retransmissions.

Assuming that the aggregate process of packet transmissions is Poisson with rate R packets per second, we calculate the probability L that a transmitted packet will be lost due to a packet collision, i.e., that a (re)transmitted packet will require retransmission. A given packet, beginning its transmission at time t, will not be interfered with if and only if no other packet transmissions begin in the interval from t-(P/C) to t+(P/C). Because the arrival process is Poisson, the probability that a packet will not experience a collision is therefore equal to the probability of no packet transmission starts for a period of 2P/C seconds. For a Poisson arrival process with mean rate R, the probability of no arrivals in 2P/C seconds (integrating the density function for t from 2P/C to infinity) is given by exp(-2R*P/ C). Thus L, the probability of a collision, is given by:

(Eq. 5-1)
$$L = 1 - e^{-2R*P/C}$$
$(0 \leq L - 1)$

With R, the channel traffic, as the steady-state mean number of transmissions per second, R*L is the number of retransmissions per second. In Abramson's basic steady-state equation, R is given as the sum of the number of retransmissions per second (R*L) and the number of new transmissions per second:

(Eq. 5-2)
$$R = N/T + R*L$$
$(0 \leq L < 1)$

Multiplying by P/C, substituting for L, and simplifying, we get an expression linking normalized channel throughput (N*P)/(C*T)) and normalized channel traffic (R*P/C), the ALOHA Result:

(Eq. 5-3)
$$\frac{N*P}{C*T} = \frac{R*P}{C} * e^{-2R*P/C}$$

The ALOHA Result indicates that the maximum normalized throughput ((N*P)/((C*T)) supported by the ALOHA channel is 1/2e channel seconds per second, corresponding to a traffic R equal to C/2P transmissions per second, a resulting probability of successful transmission 1-L equal to 1/e, and a number of users N(max):

(Eq. 5-4)
$$N(max) = \frac{C*T}{2e*P}$$

No steady-state exists for N above N(max). In physical terms, the ALOHA Result suggests that a surplus of users, above N(max), will cause the system to become unstable in a regenerative burst of retransmissions.

It is now straightforward, using parameters given us by Abramson for the ALOHA System in operation at the University of Hawaii, to evaluate N(max). C is 24 Kbps. T, the mean user "think" time, is 60 seconds. P, the packet size in bits, is the sum of (1) the number of bits required for receiver synchronization,

112 bits (or 4.67 milliseconds), (2) 32 header bits for identification and control, (3) 16 bits for header checksum, (4) 640 bits of data, and (5) 16 bits for data checksum, a total of 816 bits, corresponding to a P/C, a "tau", of 34 milliseconds. N(max) works out to be about 324 user terminals <Abramson>.

That the maximum throughput of the UHF channel is 1/2e, 18%, is not totally discouraging when we consider that the volume of output from a computer system is typically an order of magnitude higher than its input. The sequential output-return channel will saturate before the random-access input channel <Roberts2>.

The ALOHA Result Reconsidered

We now examine Abramson's analysis of the ALOHA system, not to quibble over the various simplifying assumptions of Poissonness and independence, but rather to make what we consider necessary structural changes. We introduce questionable simplifying assumptions of our own, but hope that the development thereby expedited will be worth the possible damage to our credibility.

We contend that one would not _want_ an ALOHA system to function as implied by the preceding mathematical model. The arrival of the 325th user to his ALOHA terminal should somehow not become the straw that breaks the camel's back. It would not be desirable that 324 previously happy ALOHA users be caused to lose service in an uncontrolled regenerative burst of retransmissions touched off either by the 325th user or, equivalently, a number of fast typists.

We also contend that one would not _expect_ an ALOHA system to function as implied by the preceding mathematical model. ALOHA users are presumably involved in an interaction and would not continue typing blindly ahead (generating new packets) without some results coming back. It can probably be assumed that an ALOHA terminal contains buffer space for only one or two outgoing packets. If a packet has difficulty getting successfully received at the central facility, the terminal will soon have its buffers filled and be required to "lock" its keyboard. We question the notion of modeling a user as an unquenchable Poisson source of service requests (e.g., packets) and suggest that this portion of Abramson's model be reconsidered first as we attempt to advance the analysis. Such an "infinite population" model is only appropriate for systems with subsaturation loads in which service delays have little effect on packet generation.

Time-sharing systems, and ALOHA systems alike, will continue to experience extreme peak loads; we must therefore require them to degrade smoothly when saturated. We claim that it is important to consider the behavior of an ALOHA system when it is loaded heavily, therefore to consider a "finite population" model of user behavior, and, furthermore, to look closely at system stability in saturation.

Recall that in the preceding analysis no distinction is made between the rate of a user's transmission requests and the rate of packet retransmission by his terminal. No mention is made of the terminal retransmission rate in any of the preceding calculations.

Let $1/T$ be the user's rate of new packet generation in his own virtual time (time unblocked) and let $1/G$ be the terminal's rate of packet retransmission while blocked; a "blocked" terminal or user is waiting for an acknowledgement of successful receipt of his current, pending input packet.

Assume that the amount of time a user stays unblocked is exponentially distributed with mean T.

While a user is blocked, his terminal retransmits packets at mean rate $1/G$ transmissions per second. Recall that the retransmission time should be random so as to avoid repeated retransmission collisions. Assume that retransmission intervals are exponentially distributed with mean G. Keep N as the total number of active users (unblocked or blocked) and let Q be the average number of blocked users. The aggregate transmission process is then approximately Poisson with mean rate $R=Q/G$ transmissions per second.

Note that our taking the channel traffic R to be Q/G involves what we call the "no immediate transmissions" assumption. We assume that when a packet is generated at a terminal, the terminal simply joins the retransmission process as if it has just failed to transmit its newly readied packet; the terminal does not attempt an immediate transmission as one might expect, but waits one randomly selected retransmission interval. This assumption dramatically reduces the complexity of the analysis required to revise Abramson's results. Were we to assume that a terminal attempts an immediate transmission with the generation of a new packet, then, in the following analysis, we would have to carry R as $(Q/G)+((N-Q)/T)$, to account for retransmissions and new transmissions separately. We have found that as long as T is much greater than G. the assumption we make leads to answers which approximate those of the more complex analysis. In cases where one might like to accommodate very large numbers of users, pushing the load well into saturation, G must be large, as we shall soon see. In such cases, the difference between a "no immediate transmissions" <u>model</u> and an "immediate transmissions" <u>system</u> will be significant; the following analysis will not apply.

Abramson's calculation of the probability of unsuccessful transmission, L, needs only a slight correction for our model. Given that one of the blocked terminals attempts a transmission, the rate of possibly interfering packet arrivals is not R=Q/G as Abramson's result would indicate, but rather (Q-1)/G, because there are now only Q-1 terminals in a position to transmit. With this correction to Abramson's result given in Equation 5-1, we get L=1-exp(-2* ((Q-1)/G)* P/C), for Q greater or equal to 1.

The steady-state equation which produces our revision of the ALOHA Result is based on the assumption that, in steady state, the rate at which unblocked users become blocked, i.e., the rate at which new packets are generated ((N-Q)/T), is equal to the rate at which blocked users become unblocked, i.e., the rate at which packets are successfully transmitted (R*(1-L)):

$$(\text{Eq. 5-5}) \qquad \frac{N-Q}{T} = \frac{Q}{G} * e^{\frac{-2*(Q-1)}{G} * \frac{P}{C}} \qquad (1 \leq Q \leq N)$$

As in the original ALOHA model, the traffic, R=Q/G, which supports maximum throughput is C/2P transmissions per second; we derive this result by maximizing the right side of Equation 5-5 with respect to Q. Noticing that our model assumes Q is not less than 1, we find the maximum normalized throughput of the ALOHA channel, (R*C/P)*(1-L), to be a gently decreasing function of Q, (1/2)*exp((1/Q)-1), starting at 1/2 and approaching 1/2e channel seconds per second. As one might have expected, the maximum throughput predicted by our model is slightly higher than that predicted by Abramson's modes; we do take a slightly more optimistic view of a packet's chances in the channel by subtracting its terminal from those which threaten to interfere with it. As the number of blocked terminals gets large, our relative optimism and the difference between the two results goes away, evidence the asymptotic maximum throughput of 1/2e. The probability of successful transmission at maximum throughput, (1-L)=exp((1/Q)-1), starts at 1 with Q at 1 and asymptotically approaches Abramson's result of 1/e.

Our number of users corresponding to the maximum throughput of the ALOHA channel is always larger than that calculated by Abramson (Equation 5-4):

(Eq. 5-6)
$$N(\text{max}) = \frac{C * T}{2e * P} * \left(\frac{G * e}{T} + e^{\frac{2P}{G*C}} \right)$$

If we fix the mean retransmission interval, G, at 1 second, then our new N(max) for the current ALOHA system (see the discussion immediately following Equation 5-4) evaluates to 362 users, an increase of about 11% over Abramson's. But, the new N(max) means something quite apart from the old. When the number of users exceeds N(max), the system we have modeled will function smoothly. Instead of a system collapse caused by a regenerative burst of retransmissions, users of our version of an over-loaded system will experience gradually reduced throughput and longer delays.

Note that we might well have chosen G to be, say, 10 seconds and found N(max) to be 472 users. Given any G (at least as large as 2P/C), we can calculate an N(max) -- the number of users required to achieve maximum throughput with terminals of the given G. Why not just make G large so the system can support a huge number of users at maximum throughput? The answer to this question is to be found in the following analysis of user block times. The fact is that as G grows, so too does the delay which users experience.

ALOHA Block Times

After a packet is generated by an ALOHA user, his terminal remains blocked until the packet is successfullly transmitted, i.e., until it is acknowledged. After some period, the acknowledgment arrives (with probability 1-L) or the packet is retransmitted (with probability L). L is a function of the traffic. The retransmission time-out period must be randomly chosen from a range of values to avoid repeated packet transmission collisions.

From the standpoint of mathematical tractability, a very good retransmission rule for an ALOHA terminal is that the time-out period be exponentially distributed, with mean G. The exponential distribution is desirable because (1) it supports the assumption that the aggregate retransmission process is Poisson and (2) it leads to a clean waiting time distribution. The exponential distribution is undesirable because (1) it fails to bound retransmission times from below by some positive constant to account for minimum acknowledgment time and (2) it fails to bound retransmission times from above to guarantee speedy service to a terminal user.

Recall that a packet can be (re)transmitted in P/C seconds. If we assume that packet acknowledgement time is comparable to packet transmission time and that the mean retransmission interval is much larger than either, then it is reasonable to assume that retransmission intervals are exponentially distributed. Block times are then the sum of a geometrically distributed (with mean 1/(1-L)) number of terms, each of which is exponentially distributed (with mean G much larger than P/C). The distribution of block times (b) is therefore a compound distribution <Feller> which we denote as f(b).

The Laplace transform of an exponential distribution with mean G is:

$$\text{(Eq. 5-7)} \qquad \text{LAPLACE}((1/G) * e^{-b*(1/G)}) = \frac{(1/G)}{(1/G)+s} \qquad (b \geq 0)$$

The Laplace transform of the probability density function of the sum of k identically distributed random variables is the Laplace transform of the k-fold convolution of their density, which in turn is the kth power of the Laplace transform of their density. The Laplace transform, F(s), of the probability density function of ALOHA block times, f(b), is formed from the sum of retransmission terms, each weighed by the probability of there being k retransmissions:

$$\text{(Eq. 5-8)} \qquad F(s) = \text{SUM}(k \geq 0; L^k * (1 - L) * \left(\frac{(1/G)}{(1/G)+s}\right)^{k+1}) \qquad (0 \leq L < 1)$$

Note that we continue making the "no immediate transmissions" assumption about the operation of our ALOHA system; a newly generated packet waits one random retransmission interval, even before its first transmission. This assumption accounts for the k+1 exponent in Equation 5-8; were we accounting for immediate initial transmissions, the exponent would be k, not k+1, and the following analysis would go through in much the same way.

Summing and rearranging terms we get:

$$\text{(Eq. 5-9)} \qquad F(s) = \frac{((1-L)/G)}{((1-L)/G)+s} \qquad (0 \leq L < 1)$$

We recognize from its Laplace transform that the probability density function of ALOHA block times is a negative exponential with parameter (1-L)/G. Differentiating F(s) with respect to s and evaluating at s equals zero, we get the mean ALOHA block time:

$$\text{(Eq. 5-10)} \qquad \text{Mean b} = \dot{F}(0) = \frac{G}{1-L} \qquad (0 \leq L < 1)$$

Differentiating F(s) twice and evaluating at s equals zero, we get the second moment of ALOHA waiting times from which we subtract the square of the mean to get the variance:

(Eq. 5-11) $$\text{Var } b = \frac{G^2}{(1-L)^2}$$ $(0 \leq L < 1)$

As we might expect, the expressions for the mean and variance of ALOHA block times with immediate transmissions are very similar to the above results for block times without immediate transmissions. The mean ALOHA block time with immediate transmission, for example, is simply L*G/(1-L).

We can examine the trade-off between N(max) and user block times. Using Equation 5-6, we calculated that with a G of 1 second Abramson's ALOHA system could support 362 users at maximum system throughput and that with a G of 10 seconds the system could support 472 users. Equation 5-10 tells us that a G of 1 second results in a mean user block time of 2.54 seconds at the N(max) of 362 while, with a G of 10 seconds, a user of an N(max)=472 system would suffer a mean block time of 27 seconds.

Slotted ALOHA

Roberts pointed out that ALOHA terminals could be conveniently constrained to transmit packets in synchronous slots only slightly larger than a packet time (P/C) in duration and that the maximum throughput of the ALOHA system could thereby be increased by a factor of 2 <Roberts3>.

The effect of Roberts's suggestion can be observed in either of the two preceding formulations using a revision of Abramson's result for L (Equation 5-1). We again assume that the aggregate process of packet arrivals is Poisson with rate R packets per second. A given packet which comes ready for transmission in a slot will actually enter the channel in the following slot. The given packet will escape collision only if no other packet came ready with it in the previous slot. A slot is taken to be P/C seconds long and the probability of no collision is taken to be the probability of no other arrivals in P/C seconds, approximately exp(-R*P/C). Thus, L, the probability of a collision given that a terminal sends a packet, is now:

(Eq. 5-12) $$L = 1 - e^{-R*P/C}$$ $(0 \leq L < 1)$

We note that L for the slotted ALOHA system differs from Abramson's by a factor of 2 in the exponent. By introducing the new L into the previous models, the maximum throughput increases from 1/2e to 1/e channel seconds per second -- the asymptote in our model -- corresponding to a traffic R equal to C/P packets per second, and a resulting probability of successful transmission 1-L (again) equal to 1/e.

The convenient method suggested by Roberts for achieving slot synchronization calls for terminals to begin packet transmissions only immediately after the end of a packet from the central transmitter. We observe that this simple method for slot synchronization will yield something near the factor of 2 throughput increase promised only if the propagation time to the farthest terminal (d) is negligible relative to the packet duration (P/C). To avoid collisions among packets belonging in adjacent slots, the slot time must be longer than the packet duration by at least twice the maximum propagation time, i.e., greater than (P/C)+2d. If not, then some packets from far terminals will arrive at the central receiver late enough to collide with packets from near terminals in the following slot. The throughput degradation due to the simple synchronization method will be felt, either in a higher collision rate than anticipated (above), or in longer slots and thus fewer packets per second.

It is conjectured that an optimal slot size for such a system would fall between P/C and P/C+2d seconds as a function of the distribution of propagation delays to the terminals.

A Discrete-Time Model of Slotted ALOHA

Let N be the "number" of users of an ALOHA system. Each of these users has a mean "think" time T; T is the mean time between the successful transmission of one packet and the user's generation of a next. T accounts for (1) central system service delays, (2) return transmission delays, (3) type-out time, (4) real user think time, and (5) type-in time. Each terminal sees a sequence of ALOHA slots of fixed "duration" D. When a terminal has a packet ready for transmission, it transmits that packet into the next slot with probability X (for "xmit"). (Re)transmissions repeat, in slots selected by successive Bernoulli trials each with probability X, until a packet is successfully transmitted and received.

It is (reluctantly) assumed that a sender will know of the success of a transmission before the start of the next slot. This "immediate acknowledgements" assumption, though common in ALOHA models in some form or another <Abramson1, Metcalfe9, Binder, Kleinrock2>, is somewhat damaging to the accuracy of the model. The effect of acknowledgement delay is studied briefly by Hayes and Sherman and should be given some further attention in the future <Hayes>. For our present analysis, however, we argue, as in the discussion before Equation 5-7, that the effect is negligible when the mean retransmission interval is large relative to the propagation delay between the terminals and the central system.

Summarizing:

N = "number" of users at ALOHA terminals;

T = mean "think" time of an ALOHA user;

D = slot "duration", period of global clock; and

X = probability of "xmission" given a ready packet.

For the moment, X is a given constant. User terminals attempt an unbounded number of (re)transmissions until success. X must be less than 1 if transmission collisions are to avoid indefinite repetition. X must be greater than 0 if any packets are to be sent at all.

Steady State. Take Q to be the steady-state time-average of the number of terminals with packets ready, i.e., "queued" for transmission and therefore in transmission wait. The Q users associated with these Q terminals are blocked; the passage of their virtual time is suspended.

Take W to be the steady-state time-average probability that any given slot will have exactly one packet transmission in it. W is the fraction of slots for which the central receiver will get a good packet, i.e., "win". Random noise transmission errors are ignored.

W can be calculated from Q and X in the following intuitively appealing approximate way. W is the probability that exactly 1 of the Q waiting terminals decides to transmit in a slot. A waiting terminal will attempt a (re)transmission of its ready packet in a slot with probability X and will continue waiting with probability 1-X. W corresponds to the event that 1 terminal decides to transmit (with probability X) and that Q-1 terminals continue waiting (with probability (1-X) ** (Q-1)). This event can happen in Q ways, so that:

(Eq. 5-13) $$W = Q*X*(1-X)^{Q-1}$$ $(0 \leq X < 1, 0 \leq Q \leq N)$

While this and some of the following formulations are rather simple and appealing, they are, as first pointed out to us in subsequent studies by Kleinrock and Lam <Kleinrock2>, only approximations. W should, in fact, be computed by summing, over all values of the number of queued users q, the product of the probability of finding the system with q blocked users, P(q), and the probability of exactly one transmission given q: sum(0≤q≤N; P(q)*q*X*((1-X)**(q-1))). For small X and large Q, in the range of interest, Equation 5-13 is a good approximation. The use of this approximation gives us a concise development whose results are verified later.

The "utilization" U of the channel is the fraction of slots which carry at least 1 packet. The probability of there being no packets in a slot is (1-X)**Q. Therefore:

(Eq. 5-14) $$U = 1 - (1 - X)^Q$$ (0≤X<1, 0≤Q≤N)

Summarizing :

Q = steady-state number of "queued" packets;

W = "win" probability, exactly 1 packet; and

U = "use" probability, at least 1 packet.

Slots are of duration D and the fraction of slots carrying single, and therefore successful, transmissions is W. The throughput of the channel is therefore W/D packets per second. The steady-state rate at which terminals leave transmission-wait state (i.e., leave Q) is W/D packets per second. A terminal enters user-think state with the successful transmission of a packet.

While there are Q terminals in transmission-wait (blocked) state, there are N-Q users in think state. Users leave think state by generating a new packet on the average of one every T seconds. The steady-state rate at which users enter transmission-wait state (i.e., enter Q and become blocked) by generating a packet is (N-Q)/T packets per second.

In steady-state, the rate at which terminals enter transmission-wait state equals the rate at which terminals leave transmission-wait state:

(Eq. 5-15) $$\frac{N-Q}{T} = \frac{W}{D}$$ (0≤W≤1, 0≤Q≤N)

This basic steady-state equation gives us the relation between N and Q:

(Eq. 5-16) $$N = Q + \frac{T}{D} * Q * X * (1 - X)^{Q-1}$$ (0≤X<1)
(0≤Q≤N)

Slotted ALOHA Block Times

The distribution of slotted ALOHA block times is of interest because it can provide some measure of system performance as seen by a user. Approximations of the mean and variance of the block time distribution are now calculated. Recall that block time is that time from when a packet is first generated by a user at his terminal (by hitting a carriage return key, say) until that packet is acknowledged to be successfully received at the central receiver.

Block time is computed here as the sum of (1) the time from packet generation to the start of the first slot and (2) the time through the slot containing the first successful packet. The two components of block time are assumed to be independent. It is natural to expect that the first component will be negligible relative to the second.

We assume that the times from packet generation to first slot are uniformly distributed between 0 and D seconds. This gives us a mean and variance of D/2 and (D**2)/12, respectively.

Considering the time from the start of the first slot through the slot containing the first successful packet as a function of the number of slots S required for successful transmission, we observe that S is geometrically distributed. The probability that a given terminal will both attempt and be successful with a packet transmission in any slot is X*((1-X)**(Q-1))=(W/Q) (see Equation 5-13). The probability that the S-th slot after packet generation contains the successful transmission is therefore (W/Q)*((1-(W/Q))**(S-1)), for S greater than or equal to 1. It is assumed that collision probabilities are independent of S and, in particular, that a packet's probability of collision is not higher given that it has already experienced a collision.

By adding the means and variances of the (uniformly distributed) first-slot times and the (geometrically distributed) subsequent-slot times, we get the mean and variance of slotted ALOHA block times:

(Eq. 5-17)
$$\text{Mean } B = \frac{D}{2} + \frac{D*Q}{W}$$
$(0 \le Q \le N)$
$(0 < W < 1)$

(Eq. 5-18)
$$\text{Var } B = D^2*((Q/W)^2 - (Q/W) + 1/12)$$

Fixed-X ALOHA System Stability

Our careful choice of the exponential distribution for think times and of the geometric distribution for retransmission intervals gives a system model in which the number of users instantaneously "queued", q, completely characterizes the past. If we know q at a given time, then knowledge of past q's gives us no new information about future q's. We call q "the instantaneous state" of the system. The instantaneous state q is a random variable with a time-varying distribution whose steady-state mean, Q, in particular, is a function of the number of system users N. We call Q "the state" of the system in that its value is a basic indicator of how the system is behaving. In the absence of an exact solution of the Markov chain based on q, we reason with what we already know about Q.

Imagine that we are observing an actual slotted ALOHA system in operation. We would like to know how many terminals, on the average, are blocked waiting for a successful transmission through the ALOHA channel; we would like to know Q. We choose to estimate Q by averaging over a number, say k, of our most recent observations of q. Because users are constantly joining and leaving the system, our estimate of Q, Q(k), is a moving average, moving with N. For small enough k, in fact, Q(k) is observed to drift due to the randomness in user think times and in retransmission intervals; in the extreme, Q(1) is q. As k gets very large, Q(k) approaches the Q corresponding to the current N; in the extreme, again, Q(infinity) is Q. Let us suppress k and hereafter use Q to denote our moving estimate with some k small enough to exhibit the dynamics we now consider.

For some values of Q, the average rate of terminal blocking exceeds the average rate of successful packet transmission causing Q to increase in time as the surplus of thinking users become blocked. Similarly, for some values of Q, the rate of successful transmissions exceeds the rate of terminal blocking causing Q to decrease in time as the surplus of blocked terminals transmit their packets and become unblocked. This variability in what we might call our "short term" Q is loosely formalized in an expression giving its derivative with respect to time:

(Eq. 5-19) $$\text{DERIV}(Q, t) = \frac{N-Q}{T} - \frac{W}{D}$$ $(0 \leq Q \leq N)$
$(0 \leq W \leq 1)$

Our formulation of Q's time derivative comes from allowing a disparity between the blocking rate ((N-Q)/T) and the channel throughput (W/D) formerly equated in steady-state Equation 5-15. Equation 5-19 is useful to us only insofar as it provides the sign of the time derivative of Q (as a function of Q) for our examination of stability.

Figure 5-1 is a map of an ALOHA system's state space. Using Abramson's parameter values (for T and D) we have evaluated Equation 5-19 for varying N-Q, Q, and X. The curves drawn connect the loci of so-called "steady states", i.e., those N-Q and Q pairs for which DERIV(Q,t) is zero for a given fixed X. The vertical axis gives the N-Q of a system state and is proportional to the rate of user blocking. The horizontal axis gives the Q of a system state. ALOHA systems with a given number of users N are constrained to move along lines of constant N, nearly horizontally in Figure 5-1. An intersection point of a line of constant N and a "steady-state" curve for a given fixed X corresponds to a "steady-state" Q for a system of N users with fixed xmission probability X. We are about to find that some of these "steady-state" operating points are stable and some are not.

We note in Figure 5-1 the expected behavior of steady-state throughput as a function of the number of terminals actively competing for the ALOHA channel. Starting from zero, as more terminals vie for the channel, the throughput (proportional to N-Q in steady-state) increases as the channel becomes less empty. After some Q which depends directly on the system's fixed "xmission" probability X, the steady-state throughput drops off as channel contention begins to generate excessive retransmission traffic.

Choosing a number of users, N, and a terminal "xmission" probability, X, we observe that the corresponding line of constant N and the corresponding curve of "steady-states" might intersect in one, two, or three places. (In Figure 5-1 we see only two of the possible three intersections, points A and B, for the N=400 and X=.05 system. The third intersection is to be found far off to the right and down near (N-Q)=0; not shown.) Each of these intersections defines an operating point for the given system, a point around which we might expect Q(k) to oscillate, a point corresponding to what we call a "steady-state" Q. Because system performance is so strongly dependent on Q (see Equations 5-17 and 5-18), we are immediately interested in the stability of the various steady states.

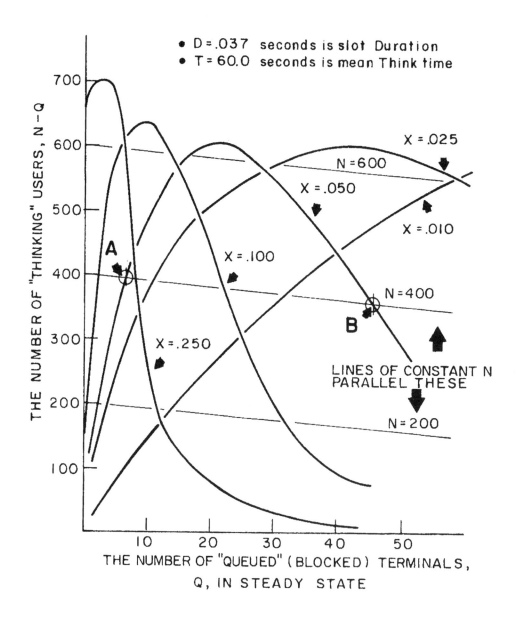

FIGURE 5-1 STEADY STATES OF FIXED-X SLOTTED ALOHA SYSTEMS

90

The stability of the various steady states is determined by considering the time derivative of Q in surrounding regions.

Our choice of axes for the graphical presentation of steady-state loci (Figure 5-1) makes it possible to determine the time derivative at a given state point by its position relative to the appropriate steady-state curve. If the point corresponding to the state in question falls above the steady-state curve, then (1) there are more thinking users than the system can support, (2) the rate of user blocking exceeds the rate of successful packet transmission, and so (3) Q can be expected to increase, moving the system state along the line of constant N out toward where that line next intercepts the curve of steady-state points. If the point falls below the steady-state curve, then (1) there are less thinking users then the system can support, (2) the rate of user blocking is less than the rate of successful packet transmission, and so (3) Q can be expected to decrease along the line of constant N in toward where that line next intercepts the curve of steady-state points.

Looking at the states for the N=400 and X=.05 system in Figure 5-1, we see that its low-Q steady state (A) is stable. The time derivative calculations for surrounding states show that the system will tend to drift back to it after small deviations due to randomness in think times and retransmissions. The next steady-state point (B) out along the line of N=400 users, is not stable. The surrounding states are found to have Q time derivatives which would bring the system farther away from it after any small deviation. The high-Q steady-state (not shown in Figure 5-1) is also found to be stable.

We conclude that a fixed-X slotted ALOHA system may have two stable steady states. Of these, the low-Q stable steady state is desirable because the mean and variance of the block time distribution are smaller. As the number of users of a given ALOHA system increases, i.e., as the line of constant N is moved up, the possibility of falling into the undesirable high-Q stable, steady state increases. As the line of constant N is moved up, the low-Q stable state is moved closer to the mid-Q unstable state and, therefore, the probability that Q(k) will drift out past the mid-Q state increases; once past the mid-Q state, Q(k) will tend to continue drifting out toward the high-Q stable steady state.

Fixed-X ALOHA Systems Compared

It is evident from Figure 5-1 that the performance of a slotted ALOHA system is strongly dependent on X, the probability that a terminal (re)transmits into a slot given it has a ready packet. This dependence is not observable in Abramson's simpler ALOHA model; we have, however, seen a similar dependence in the discussion surrounding Equation 5-10. The mean retransmission interval, G, given in our earlier analysis, played a role similar to that played by the mean retransmission interval calculable in this analysis, (D/X)-D.

We hint at a subsequent development of our model by calling the systems studied in Figure 5-1 "fixed-X" ALOHA systems.

The dependence of system performance on X is characterized by a trade-off between light loading performance and heavy loading performance. For large X (near 1), a lightly loaded system operates at very low Q with correspondingly low block times. But, as N increases, the relative stability of the low-Q stable, steady state drops off quickly and the probability of the system's falling into the low performance high-Q stable steady state increases -- the system bogs down in retransmissions. In short, the system behaves much like a system conforming to Abramson's model. But, for small X, a lightly loaded system operates at a much higher Q and offers accordingly higher block times; as N increases, however, the system resists falling into its high-Q stable steady state and degrades performance smoothly.

The steady-state throughput, W/D packets per second, is a function of the slot duration D, the steady-state mean number of (re)transmitting terminals Q, and the "xmission probability" X (see Equation 5-13). Differentiating W/D with respect to X, setting equal to zero, and solving for X, we get that value of X which maximizes throughput for a given Q:

(Eq. 5-20) $$X' = \frac{1}{Q}$$ (0<X<1)

(1<Q<N)

Looking back at Figure 5-1 we see that the steady-state (throughput) curves peak out at the Q equal to the reciprocal of their respective X's. From this we can infer that an ALOHA system operating at some Q would be best off if its X were equal to 1/Q. And from this we might conclude that some consideration be given to changing X as a function of Q.

With the beginnings of a slotted ALOHA system control strategy in hand, we are now obliged to go back to the model for a more rigorous investigation; in particular, we need to show that our approximate Q-based reasoning can be supported by exact reasoning on the instantaneous system state q.

If the slotted ALOHA system has q blocked terminals at the end of a slot, then what is the distribution of q+, the number of blocked terminals at the end of the next slot? There are two independent q-controlled random processes which combine to determine q+. These are the terminal blocking process of Poisson rate (N-q)/T and the packet transmission process, an ALOHA aggregate of q Bernoulli trials.

The number of terminals that become blocked in a slot of D seconds is Poisson distributed with expectation (N-q)*(D/T); the number that become unblocked in a slot is either 0 or 1, the latter with probability q*X* ((1 - X)** (q - 1)), as found for Q in the straightforward arguments leading to Equation 5-13. The expectation of q+ is therefore:

$$\text{(Eq. 5-21)} \qquad E(q+) = q + (N - q) * \frac{D}{T} - q * X * (1 - X)^{q-1}$$

From our Q-based arguments leading to Equation 5-20, we note at once that taking X as the reciprocal of q minimizes the expectation of q+. If it were possible to maintain X at 1/q, then the probability of successful transmission would be maximized, the throughput maximized, and the expectation of q minimized, in each slot.

It is possible to construct a slotted ALOHA system in which X is controlled as function of system state. Two basic problems must be solved. First, it must be determined whether X should be controlled by the central transceiver or by each of the terminals independently. Second, q must be estimated.

If the central transceiver is to control X, then a control field in outgoing messages or a control message must be defined with which the central transceiver can notify terminals of the optimal "xmission" probability. If the terminals are to compute X themselves, then they must be slightly more complex than either the currently operational ALOHA terminals or Roberts's hand-held personal terminal.

To determine the optimal "xmission" probability X, either the central transceiver or each of the terminals must maintain an estimate of q. One practical solution is to maintain a moving estimate of channel utilization U (the fraction of slots in which at least one packet is transmitted) which, with a knowledge of the current setting of X, gives Q using Equation 5-14. An estimate of W might be easier to keep; W and the current X give Q using Equation 5-13. In either case, Q's reciprocal, as argued up to Equation 5-20, will serve as the throughput maximizing X.

As the number of terminals contending for the ALOHA channel increases, the terminals should lower their retransmission rate to share the channel optimally. In an ALOHA system, straightforward local optimization would lead to global catastrophe: if terminals increased their retransmission rate in the face of decreasing success probabilities, the terminals would collapse communications totally. By cooperating, "optimal" sharing of the channel can be achieved. It is reasonable to expect terminals to cooperate in traffic-based retransmission control because it is already assumed that terminals will not jam the channel and, in fact, will observe slot boundaries.

We have not determined how often X must be updated to keep a controlled-X slotted ALOHA system near maximal throughput. Neither have we determined whether controlling X will lead to stable system performance.

Controlled-X ALOHA System Stability

Now assume that the terminals in a slotted ALOHA system are able to adjust their "xmission" probability X and assume that X is thereby continuously equal to 1/q. We ignore the fact that terminals must estimate Q over some interval and that there may be some dynamics in the system's response to inaccurate X adjustments. Replacing X by 1/Q in Equation 5-16 and rearranging, we get:

$$\text{(Eq. 5-22)} \qquad N - Q = \frac{T}{D} * (1 - \frac{1}{Q})^{Q-1} \qquad (1 \le Q \le N)$$

Superimposing the curve defined by Equation 5-22 over those shown in Figure 5-1, we get Figure 5-2 showing the dominance of the controlled-X system over the various fixed-X systems. Rather than reaching a maximum at some Q above 1 as for the fixed-X systems, the controlled-X system's steady-state throughput, (N–Q)/T, begins at 1/D packets per second with Q=1 and decreases monotonically to 1/(D*e) as Q goes to infinity.

Our formulation fails to inform us about steady-state throughput for Q below 1, but we must presume that it peaks below 1 and goes to 0 with Q. Then, we observe that the controlled-X slotted ALOHA system has one, very low-Q, stable steady state for a wide range of N's. As the number of users, N, grows past T/(D*e) and moves the system into what might be called "saturation", the line of constant N finally intersects with the controlled-X system's steady-state

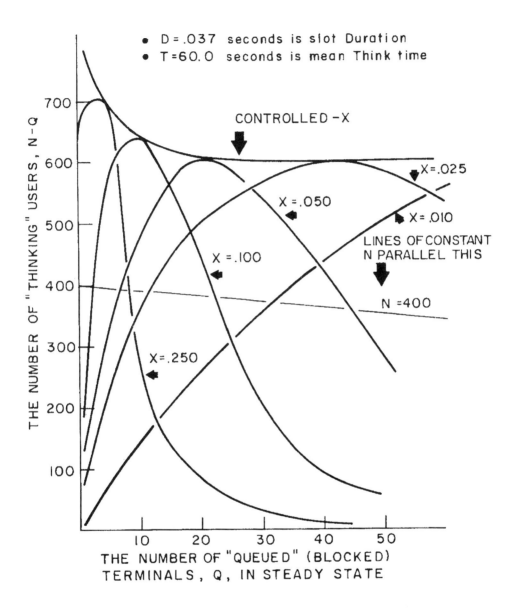

FIGURE 5-2 STEADY STATES OF A CONTROLLED-X SLOTTED ALOHA SYSTEM

curve out where Q is much larger than 1; a high-Q stable steady state does develop, but at a much lower Q than any fixed-X system.

Recall (from Equation 5-14) our expression for steady-state slotted ALOHA utilization, U. Assuming X controlled to be continuously equal to 1/Q, we see that U approaches a limit of 1-(1/e) or about 63% as Q goes (with N) to infinity.

Similarly, we see (from Equation 5-13) that W, the probability of a successful transmission in a slot, approaches a limit of 1/e or about 37% as Q goes (with N) to infinity.

As rules of thumb we propose that in a heavily loaded, slotted, and controlled ALOHA system, 63% of the slots will contain at least one packet, 37% will contain exactly one packet, and, therefore, 26% will contain multiple, interfering packets.

The controlled-X system has the feature that, as new users become active, the steady-state throughput, (N-Q)/T, approaches a non-zero limit. As more and more users push the system into saturation, the aggregate rate of "thinking" ((N-Q), say) stays constant as the active terminals take less of the channel and remain blocked a larger fraction of the time. In fixed-X systems, however, new users joining the system in saturation reduce the aggregate rate of thinking; they have a negative marginal product.

Up to this point in the report, we have studied various techniques relating to the use of computing in packet communication systems. In the next and final chapter, we turn briefly to look at the impact of packet communication on the organization of computing systems.

Best-Efforts Thin-Wire
Interprocess Communication

Computer communication is, again, both communication <u>using</u> computers and communication <u>among</u> computers. Thus far in the report, we have analyzed certain techniques for the application of computing in communication; in this final chapter, we turn to consider communication in computing -- structures for organizing computers in highly communicative environments.

Let there be no doubt that we consider this chapter to be speculative, i.e., the kind of material one needs <u>before</u> setting out to prove something; while our experience in computing and packet communication leaves us enthusiastic about some of the notions to be presented, we recognize them as little more than feelings and invite the reader to examine them in this light.

Summary

A recurring problem in the development of the ARPANET has been the coordination of remote processes. Any one of a number of existing schemes for interprocess communication might have been expected to offer itself as a ready solution, but, the fact is, the basic organization of ARPANET interprocess communication -- a general-purpose HOST-HOST protocol -- was long in coming and troublesome when it arrived. At the time of the Network Working Group's decision to adopt the current "official" HOST-HOST protocol, two specific proposals were considered: one based on connections <Crocker1> and the other on messages <Walden> (see Appendix B). The earlier proposal, based on connections, was chosen, we believe, because connections, much more than messages, resemble structures in familiar, centralized computer operating systems.

We believe, in retrospect, that Walden's early proposal would have been the better choice -- that the underlying structures of ARPANET interprocess communication should be modeled, not after the centralized computing systems they join, but after the distributed packet-switching system they use. ARPANET experience leads us to suggest that there are valuable distinctions to be made between (1) <u>centralized</u> interprocess communication techniques as often employed within computer operating systems <Eastlake, Lampson, Poupon, Saltzer, Schroeder> and (2) <u>distributed</u> interprocess communication techniques as required in computer networks <Akkoyunlu, Bressler, Bressler1, Farber, Kalin1, Rutledge, Schaffner, Thomas1, Walden>. These distinctions bring us to propose that even the latest plans to develop a message-based distributed interprocess communication system for the ARPANET, especially floating "ports" and generalized "rendezvous" <Bressler1>, are not extreme enough in their departure from techniques used in centralized computing systems.

We propose that so-called "thin-wire" strategies for interprocess communication be used more generally within and among computer systems because thin-wire interprocess communication (1) has a clarifying effect on the management of multiprocess activity and (2) generalizes well as computer systems become more distributed. We further propose that so-called "best-efforts" strategies be used more generally because best-efforts interprocess communication (1) takes fullest advantage of the potential for error recovery found in highly error-prone distributed environments and (2) encourages the economic distribution of reliability mechanisms in large systems.

The thrust of our proposal is in opposition to that most often offered by those studying organizations of distributed computing systems:

> All elements of a distributed system should be accessible
> as if <u>local</u> to one another.

By arguing that best-efforts thin-wire interprocess communication should be more generally applied, we propose:

> All elements of a distributed system should be accessible
> as if <u>remote</u> from one another.

We begin with a short statement of what role "processes" play in computing and attempt to show that it is no longer necessary to compromise on the formal notion of process in the actual building of computer systems, especially now that processing itself is so inexpensive. Then, we characterize the basic problems one solves in developing protocols for interprocess communication and try to underscore the differences between techniques used in centralized and distributed computing environments. We develop some of the features of using "thin-wire" communication in the management of multiprocess activity and, finally, we point out some of the virtues of a "best-efforts" philosophy in the building of distributed systems.

Processes

The word "process" is used widely and has varying technical meaning <Fisher, Lampson, Saltzer, Thomas, Vyssotsky>. For our purposes, a process is a program in execution on a virtual machine: a processor, some procedure, data, and (now) communication ports <Akkoyunlu, Balzer, Schaffner>. A process is a formal object <Fisher, Habermann, Thomas> which is appropriate for personification and, therefore, useful as an aid to thinking about computer systems.

One can think about the process handling the management of an operating systems's disk hardware -- i e., the disk process. One can think about the process managing the execution of a certain user program -- i.e., a job. The disk process and a job must cooperate to carry data between the job's address space (e.g., mapped central memory) and the disk process's address space (e.g., physical disk blocks). It is often useful to view a job and the disk manager as distinct processes simply because disks (or tapes or terminals or printers) run asynchronously with respect to other system devices and need to be managed (at some level) in an asynchronously evolving context <Walden>.

Operating systems seldom handle processes in a clean and uniform way. Many designs have internal system processes (e.g., disk processes) "embedded" in a monolithic supervisor and scheduled by special priority interrupt hardware, while jobs (i.e., user processes) are scheduled through an entirely different mechanism in software <Metcalfe4>.

Embedded system processes typically run in "supervisor mode" and share wide access to central memory, while jobs run in "user mode" and are carefully confined in their memory accesses by address mapping and validation hardware. Embedded system processes themselves often have no particular uniformity, each being carefully tailored to a specific high-priority task.

Such non-uniform organizations of process management are often justified with compelling arguments relating to the efficient multiplexing of processing units: processes which must run in frequent, short bursts cannot be subject to the scheduling overhead normally associated with jobs, i.e., with formally manipulable processes. But, we contend, these short-cuts around scheduling overhead, besides prohibiting the transfer of system functions to other nodes in some computer network, spoil otherwise intuitively structured designs and, therefore, obstruct system development and maintenance. Informal and non-uniform treatment of processes leads to a proliferation of confused interprocess communication techniques and to resulting elusive malfunctions.

In current computer systems, the quantity of processor state information (dynamic context) associated with formally manipulable processes is high, especially in systems with non-trivial memory mapping (e.g., Multics, Tenex, TSS) <Deutsch>. The most convincing arguments against more systematic handling of processes are founded on the high costs of context switching in the multiplexing of a central processor among many processes <Lampson>. Improved hardware (e.g., faster processors, faster memory, context-switching devices) is reducing these costs. Now, the contortions required to multiplex a few large "processes" over many unrelated functions and across access-control boundaries (i.e., domains <Lampson>) are becoming relatively significant <Schroeder>.

In short, recent advances in processor technology, especially in cost reduction, make it possible to avoid the burden of multiplexing a large central processor among a large population of processes; many formally managed processes, some even with their own dedicated processors, can now be used liberally in more intuitively appealing organizations of computing activity.

Protocols for Interprocess Communication

The ways in which processes organize their (local or remote) cooperation are called "protocols". We use the word to refer to a set of agreements among communicating processes relating to (1) rendezvous (who and where), (2) format (what and how), and (3) timing (when) of data and control exchanges.

We see at least four problem areas in which protocol agreements must be made: (1) routing, (2) flow, (3) congestion, and (4) security.

Routing. Interdependent processes must be able to find one another (rendezvous) in an interprocess (centralized or distributed) communication system and their data exchanges appropriately routed. Routing may involve something as simple as a publicized memory address, or a rendezvous protocol <Postel1>, or perhaps even considerations of a dynamic topology in a packet switching network <Heart>; in the latter case, routing has implications for flow and congestion <Fultz, Zeigler>.

Flow. Once communicating, processes must be able to control the flow of data among them. Processing-power mismatches and varying load make it probable that some processes will fall behind in their handling of data exchanges; this falling behind must be managed. Queues and buffers are often used to cushion flow mismatches <Habermann>. Allocation schemes, by coordinating communication and computing, are helpful in keeping data from clogging a communication system when a receiver of data lags behind its sender <McKenzie1>.

Congestion. The multiplexing of a communications facility over a population of communicating processes requires methods for assuring equitable access. While communicating processes may be handling their own flow control problems via some private protocol, the communications substrate must assume the responsibility of balancing the use of communication resources among various ongoing interactions. Congestion in the communication system must be controlled so that heavy flow among certain processes does not block effective interaction among others <Kahn4>.

Security. In the sense we use it, the word "security" carries with it our concern for both reliability and privacy. Large systems should not be built with the assumption that all components will function smoothly all of the time <Kalin2>. If increasingly distributed systems are to be increasingly effective, they must be built to respond robustly to errors. Interprocess communication protocols must provide for maximally resilient error recovery. Table redundancy, consistency checking, retransmissions, acknowledgments, and time-outs are familiar techniques for the support of contingency handling.

As communicators become more distant, the growing concern for security from transmission error must be accompanied by efforts to protect against less random intervention, namely unauthorized access <Lampson1>. Redundancy and encryption are techniques for controlling access to communicated data <PCI>.

Centralized Protocols

In a centralized computing environment, cooperating processes are near to one another (in time and space) and to a shared central memory. A protocol for interprocess communication in a centralized environment often takes the form of a set of rules governing the addressing of shared memory (e.g., core, disk), the layout of tables and queues therein, and the coordination of data access and modification <Habermann, Walden>.

In the centralized environment, embedded system processes often have wide access to system data bases, including many unrelated to their separate functions. Such processes, often organized in an ad hoc manner for high efficiency, are somewhat prone to malfunction; and, because their access to shared data is largely unconstrained in central memory, intermittent interactions among unrelated processes are common, making computer operating system development and maintenance a recurring nightmare.

It will continue to be important to look for ways to intelligently constrain various components of computing systems toward reducing the probability of subtle, unintentional interactions in shared memory; we look to the developers of system implementation languages for such help (e.g., <Wegbreit>). As we will soon argue, an additional aid to controlling the reliable operation of large computer systems is to be found in the strict isolation of their component processes through the exclusive use of highly constrained, thin-wire, interprocess communication.

Distributed Protocols

In one sense all processes are remote from one another; it is just that some processes are more remote than others. We begin to have distributed computing environments when the distance in space or time between components becomes a factor in basic organization. If two processes share a central memory, but the central memory requires a million instruction times to access, then we can say that, despite the central memory, the processes are remote; indeed, we might usefully view the central memory as yet a third process and references to it as message exchanges over a communication channel.

Protocols for distributed interprocess communication do not deal with tables and queues in a shared central memory, but rather with explicit data exchange. Messages are sent and acknowledgments (ACKs) received, inquiries received and data returned, probes launched and responses recorded or timed-out. In short, the essence of distributed interprocess communication is dealing with a high degree of isolation and uncertainty.

Protocols for distributed interprocess communication are influenced most by the requirement for concise communication. Conciseness is achieved (1) by careful <u>partitioning</u> of data among processes so as to minimize data exchanges and (2) by mechanisms for high <u>selectivity</u>. A premium must be placed on keeping data where it is to be most often accessed, and communication must be organized around to-the-point data exchanges.

Communicating processes in a distributed environment must coordinate themselves using data exchanges squeezed through relatively long and narrow data paths -- as if joined only by thin wires. Therefore, we refer to techniques that show the effects of optimization for the use of such data paths as "thin-wire" techniques for interprocess communication. Such techniques tend to be based on explicit, sequential, low bandwidth, and high delay data exchanges.

Patterns in human communication parallel those of processes. When in the same room, people communicate via protocols with high redundancy using a large repertoire of sounds, faces, and gesticulations. By mail or over a telephone, people have more constrained, serial protocols (i.e., thin-wire protocols) which, though painful on occasion, give considerably increased access to large and distributed audiences. People keep lists of commonly used telephone numbers on their person or by their phone; an example of everyday data partitioning. People seldom have the entire telephone directory read to them by the information operator; an example of everyday data selectivity.

Centralized versus Distributed

Centralized and distributed communications environments can be contrasted on (1) transmission rate, (2) transmission delay, (3) reliability, and (4) explicitness of data exchange.

<u>Transmission Rate.</u> In a centralized environment, data rates (in bits per second) are limited only by the speed of central memory and are often high in the Mbps (megabits per second) range. As processes become separated by long thin wires and intermediate processing points, data rates drop orders of magnitude into the Kbps range and lower.

For the small packets often exchanged by cooperating processes, the reduced transmission rates in distributing environments can be ignored, but for repeated bulk transfers, local communication is desirable. Careful data partitioning and high selectivity can reduce the need for bulk transfers. Data transmission rates can be expected to increase dramatically with emerging communication technology.

Transmission Delay. Transmission delay is a critical parameter of interprocess communication in that delays cause processes to be idle. Superficially, the delays in central systems are in the nanosecond range and contrast significantly with the millisecond and second delays in the ARPANET, for example, not to mention the second, minute, and hour delays of more conventional computer communication systems.

The transmission delays of computer communication networks will continue to fall. In accessing shared data in the central environment, the significant transmission delays are those imposed by multiprocess locking of shared data <Madnick> and by scheduling delays of processes in a multiplexed processor environment.

In addition to geographical separation, relatively low transfer rates and high delays make distributed systems distributed.

Reliability. A most important contrast to be drawn between centralized and distributed computing is that of reliability. When a disk controller sends a buffer to a user job, it is assumed that the transfer will complete successfully. When the transfer fails, the operating system typically initiates some drastic procedure (e.g., halt) until the difficulty is found and fixed. The malfunction of even a single bit in a single word of a computer system's central memory may lead to a total collapse.

In a distributed computing system, errors are the rule. Because distributed systems are constructed by many different people at many different times, the potential for malfunction is considerably higher than that of centralized systems; the potential for error recovery in distributed systems is, fortunately, also very high. Because remote processes have only their communications in common (and not their memory and processor) the malfunction of one does not necessarily lead to the death of some other. Remote processes can detect malfunctions in each other and attempt to recover gracefully. It is not hard to imagine situations in which a malfunction might cause communicating processes to seek alternative processing while initiating action for test and repair.

Explicitness. When communicating processes exchange data through a shared central memory, one process usually discovers that its data base has been updated by another. If the update is properly timed and of the appropriate format, the communication results in cooperation; in the all too frequent case that the update comes intermittently out of sequence or from a completely unexpected source as garbage, the communication results in chaos.

When a data exchange is made over a thin wire, the sender must consciously (explicitly) select the data and transmit it. The receiver must consciously (explicitly) receive the data and dispense with it. There is no opportunity for one process to clobber another's domain without its explicit consent and active cooperation. Processes can be arbitrarily scrutinizing of explicitly communicated data and can thereby defend themselves against either malfunction or malice.

Thin-Wire Interprocess Communication

In the ARPANET, IMPs connected by 50 Kbps telephone circuits (i.e., thin wires) use an IMP-IMP protocol in cooperating to perform transmission error control, congestion control, and packet routing. The IMP Subnet provides communication links (thin wires) among HOST computers. The "official" general purpose HOST-HOST protocol organizes the cooperation of HOST computers through links, creating a system of virtual JOB-JOB connections (thin wires again). Each of these levels (i.e., IMP-IMP, HOST-HOST, and JOB-JOB) involves the cooperation of processes (i.e., IMPs, HOSTs , and JOBs) using data exchanges through thin wires (i.e., circuits, links, and connections).

In trying to understand thin-wire interprocess communication, we first recognize that communication systems (e.g., the ARPANET, above) can have levels of organization, some connection-oriented or circuit-oriented, and some message-oriented or packet-oriented, forming a system of hierarchically arranged virtual levels sharing a common hardware base.

For the moment, we choose the word connection to identify a path carrying a sequence of data exchanges between processes. Some connections correspond to physical communication channels (circuits), while others are simply sequences of table transactions: ARPANET communication computers (IMPs) are connected by 50 Kbps telephone circuits, while ARPANET user JOBs can be joined via the virtual connection system created by ARPANET Network Control Programs (NCPs) <Carr>.

The methods by which processes become connected vary. IMPs become connected when their attached circuits are observed to be functioning. ARPANET user JOBs establish connections through acknowledged requests on the ARPANET's NCP-supported virtual connection system. Connection systems typically handle flow, congestion, and error control internally and seldom bother communicating processes with the details.

A <u>packet</u> is a self-contained data exchange. When a packet first enters a communication system, its size, source, destination, and priority, for example, enter with it; when it leaves that communication system, so do they and other traces specific to it. A communication system that deals in packets is not required to dedicate resources to a certain packet until the actual moment of its arrival; the allocation of resources is (almost) purely on demand.

A packet is a virtual object. Some packets are actual bit sequences through a communication channel and others are formal objects, either constructed in a centralized environment simulating a channel, or subdivided into physical units (like segments into pages) <Saltzer>.

Because each packet contains the full specification of an exchange between sender and receiver, large exchanges requiring multiple packets to carry them will have that full specification repeated in each of the packets. In cases where data flows are voluminous, the per-packet overhead will make for poor utilization of communication facilities. A connection, on the other hand, is begun with the setting up of state information in a communication system so that transmissions via the connection need not contain repetitions of, say, the rendezvous specifications exchanged at connect time. In cases where data flow is voluminous, a connection is a very effective way of utilizing communications resources because the setup costs are amortized over a large number of streamlined transmissions. If the traffic among processes is predominantly light and bursty, however, then the relatively high connection setup costs will dominate and efficiency will be low. The creation of a connection corresponds to the dedication of same resources to an interprocess communication. To the extent that the communication over a connection is sporadic, the dedicated resources are wasted.

Thin-wire interprocess communication techniques, be they through a circuit or packet switching system, are a significant departure from those techniques for centralized computer system communication with which we are all more familiar. For detailed examples of various thin-wire techniques, refer to the abundant documentation of ARPANET protocols <McKenzie1, Postel, Postel1, Bhushan, Bhushan6, Michener, Kalin1, Bressler1>. To highlight some of the more fundamental characteristics of such techniques requires only a few words: (1) format standards, (2) sequencing, (3) flow control, (4) access control, and (5) best-efforts reliability.

Because processes which cooperate via thin wires tend to be running in different machines or are designed to do so, thin-wire techniques exhibit the effects of considerable care in the selection of data formats and representations. Knowing that a process at the far end of a thin wire need only have its communication facilities in common with the process at the near end -- not its processor, memory sizes, or manufacturer -- the designers of thin-wire protocol find it incumbent upon them to choose formats for data exchanges which are somewhat general and natural to their purpose <Bhushan>.

Because processes joined only by thin wires tend to run by different clocks and suffer from variable delay between them, thin-wire techniques show recurrent concern for synchronization and sequencing. Data exchanges are often specified in inquiry/response pairs and, especially at start up, these pairs serve to bring distant communicators into phase with one another. One common characteristic of such pairs is that the inquiry and response are identical so as to suppress the relative timing of their transmissions in symmetric cooperation <Postel1, McKenzie1, Burchfiel, Kalin1>. When, for reliability, data exchanges are marked with sequence numbers, as they often are, it is usual that an inquiry/response pair will be defined to allow the processes to get back into sequence in the event of a lost exchange <Bhushan6, BBN1822>.

Because distant processes differ in their ability to generate and process data, flow control mechanisms are common in thin-wire protocols. Often, a certain message from one process to another is taken as an indication of newly allocated message buffer space, i.e., a permission to send data to a process which has indicated its ability to accept them. There are examples of interprocess messages which signify the reduction of a previous allocation by a specified amount, but those deallocation messages that have proven most useful ask a sending process to send no more data until a new allocation is received <McKenzie1, Burchfiel, Salin1>.

Because thin-wire techniques usually require the explicit generation, transmission, reception, and discard of communicated data, interprocess access control is an almost automatic feature of distributed interprocess communication. Processes can, indeed, be arbitrarily scrutinizing of explicitly transmitted data and can thereby defend themselves against either malfunction or malice. Communication over a thin wire is something a secretive process can do freely, in much the same way that people freely use their telephones in varying stages of undress. Thin wires can provide a medium for cooperation among embittered, mutually suspicious subsystems <Lampson>. While the appropriate primitive is provided in the ARPANET -- the IMP Subnet guarantees the correct identification of a message's source HOST -- little use has been made of thin-wire interprocess access control <BBN1822, Postel1>.

And now, finally, best-efforts thin-wire reliability.

Large and, especially, distributed systems are a reliability problem <Kalin2>. Unfortunately, the most effective way to achieve reliability these days is through stability -- inertia in development. But isn't distributed computing supposed to help reliability?

As we have previously indicated, processes at the far ends of a thin wire both are hurt by and benefit from their relative isolation. They are hurt because the thin wire limits the rate at which they can exchange bits; they benefit because the thin wire limits the extent to which a malfunction at one end need result in a malfunction at the other.

A system which depends jointly on a large number of its components to sustain operation will have poor reliability for the simple reason that the unreliability of the components will accumulate multiplicatively in the unreliability of the system. Whereas thin wires provide the potential for component isolation in distributed systems and thereby the potential for continued system operation in the face of component failure, only intercomponent protocols which are both sensitive and responsive to component failure can hope to realize the potential of thin-wire isolation; such failure-responsive protocols are the essence of what we call the "best efforts" philosophy of interprocess communication.

Imagine that we are a component process in the midst of some large system. There are two extreme attitudes we might have toward the system and toward the several component processes upon which we depend. We might believe the processes around us to be so reliable, irreplaceable, and interdependent that, if one should fail, there would be little point in trying to carry on. Or, we might believe the processes around us to be so unreliable, expendable, and independent that, if some should fail, there would be considerable potential in our being able to patch things up to struggle on, weakened, but doing our job. This second attitude is characteristic of what we call the "best efforts" philosophy of interprocess communication; it is based on our desire to give the system our best efforts and, to do so, on our expecting only as much from the processes upon which we depend.

ARPANET IMPs, for example, treat telephone circuits as unreliable, expendable, independent components of the packet-switching system. Telephone circuits are individually asked to give their best efforts to the transmission of digital data. Realizing that a telephone circuit's best is not perfect, the IMPs take steps to monitor circuit performance and, detecting a malfunction, to retry, and, failing some number of retrys, to take alternative action, namely to use alternate paths to get packets closer to their destination. Beyond this, the IMPs are suspicious of one another and can recover in various ways to provide partial service in the face of IMP failures.

You will note that the ability to recover from partial malfunction doesn't always require what might be called "pure redundancy"; a reliable system doesn't necessarily require duplicate components sitting idly by, waiting for failure. The ARPANET's telephone circuits are a good example. When they are all working properly, the circuits combine to provide a high total transmission capacity, perhaps slightly higher than the network might otherwise require. When some circuits go down, those remaining continue transmission service, but at a reduced total capacity .

Of course, best-efforts techniques have been around for some time; for example, take the familiar retry procedures used in reading magnetic tape. But now, with computers, the best-efforts philosophy can be applied pervasively in large systems. Computers contribute by providing component isolation through computer communication and by providing "distributed intelligence" with which to implement non-trivial error-detection and recovery mechanisms wherever appropriate <Chen>.

But why make an issue out of something as simple as this "best-efforts" idea? Why call it a philosophy? Why give it a name at all? For the simple reason that, without a conscious effort to do otherwise, computer people (especially) find it easy to neglect the potential offered by thin-wire isolation -- they've worked in centralized environments for so long.

As evidence to support this proposition, take experience with the ARPANET again (see Appendices A and B). With a few minor exceptions (e.g., the lack of error-detection in IMP memories and the IMP-HOST interface), the IMP Subnet shows the failure-tolerance to be derived from the best-efforts philosophy conscientiously applied by people working close to communications hardware they know to be faulty. The history of the "official" HOST-HOST protocol, on the other hand, shows the consistent fragility of techniques invented for distributed interprocess communication by people working with the delicate innards of computer operating systems.

If we can develop and use thin-wire techniques for interprocess communication, then as computing environments become more distributed, our systems will generalize. In the meantime, a formal organization of process management and interprocess communication will aid in making systems work. If we can develop and use strategies for best-efforts interprocess communication, then we can take fullest advantage of the potential for error-recovery found in highly error-prone distributed environments and encourage the economic distribution of reliability mechanisms in large systems.

Appendix A
The ARPANET
Communications Subnet

The workings of the ARPANET are, as will become apparent in the following two appendices, startlingly simple. Were it not that the ARPANET already links over 30 centers of computing activity across the USA, it would be very hard to believe that its simple packet communication techniques could work at all. But the ARPANET does work; and to such an extent that a commercial version on a grand scale is imminent <PCI>. While we might already be curious about why the ARPANET works as well as it does, thinking about an impending world-wide digital communications utility makes us feel a certain urgency to understand what is essential in the techniques and, as is the purpose of this report, to fit the essentials into a theory of packet communication.

The simplicity of the packet communication techniques used in the ARPANET makes it easy to describe them in some detail and, thereby, to substantiate the theories to which they give rise. We hope that the following pages of tutorial description will prove helpful, but keep in mind that much of the material appears elsewhere, if not more clearly, at least at greater length.

This first of two tutorial appendices gets into the internal mechanisms of the ARPANET's subnetwork of packet-switching communications computers (i.e., IMPs), developed and maintained by Bolt Beranek and Newman Inc., Cambridge, Massachusetts (BBN). BBN has produced a number of documents which must be studied for a thorough understanding of the packet communication techniques surveyed here <BBN1822, Heart, McKenzie, Mimno, Ornstein>.

The IMP-HOST Interface

The ARPANET, as we often emphasize, involves both communication <u>among</u> computers and communication <u>using</u> computers; among things called "HOSTs" using things called "IMPs". The subnetwork of IMPs provides a core of communications functions; without the IMPs, these functions would need costly replication in each of the various HOSTs. A HOST communicates with other HOSTs, not directly, but rather through a local IMP which acts on its behalf in the realm of IMPS to get messages transmitted (see Figure 7-1).

For reasons of maintainability and reliability, IMPs are essentially identical -- it would be better if they were exactly identical. HOSTs, however, are not all the same; in fact, as a result of their prior isolation, they are bashful of one another and often seemingly hostile. From our standpoint, it is the similarities among HOSTs which would be important in coming to grips with the mechanisms of packet communication, but it is the differences which one first sees.

Therefore, we begin by looking into the IMP Subnet as if one were a HOST, rather than the opposite. In this appendix we venture into the IMP Subnet; later, in the next appendix, we look at the structures which evolve inside HOSTs to deal with the IMPs and through them with distant HOSTs.

That which physically joins a HOST computer (e.g., a PDP-10, a 360/91, a Sigma-7) to its IMP (Interface Message Processor) is, at its narrowest part, a 12-wire cable sustaining bi-directional, bit-serial, asynchronous message communication. At one end of this cable is the IMP's "general" IMP-HOST interface and at the other end is the HOST's "special" IMP-HOST interface <BBN1822>. Traffic across the IMP-HOST interface is limited to messages of at most 8095 bits at a maximum rate of 100 kilobits per second (Kbps) each way. IMP-HOST message exchanges are presumed to be error-free.

The "standard" IMP-HOST interface requires that the IMP-HOST cable be shorter than 30 feet. There is a "distant" IMP-HOST interface which permits cable lengths up to 2000 feet. The limitations on cable length are due (1) to the requirement that IMP-HOST transmissions be error-free and (2) to the fact that long cables cause delays which significantly degrade maximum IMP-HOST bit-rate, under the bit-by-bit, asynchronous hand-shake transmission scheme used. For IMP-HOST connections longer than 2000 feet, BBN offers a "very distant" IMP-HOST interface providing retransmission-based, IMP-IMP-like, error-checked, telephone circuit communication <BBN1822>.

The 12-wire IMP-HOST cable carries two 6-wire signal sets, one for

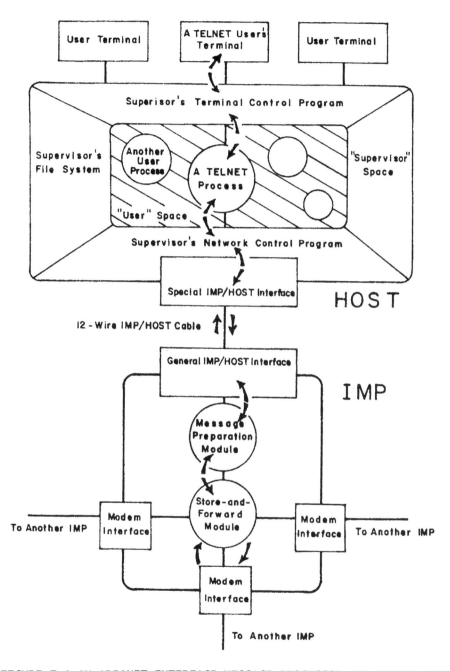

FIGURE 7-1 AN ARPANET INTERFACE MESSAGE PROCESSOR AND TELNET USER

IMP-to-HOST data and one for HOST-to-IMP data. The two 6-wire sets are symmetrical so that by appropriately cross connecting (i.e., by looping or cross-patching), either the IMP or the HOST can independently test its transmission hardware and the cable. The interfaces that we (i.e., the author) constructed for the MIT Project MAC DMCG PDP-10 and the Xerox PARC MAXC HOST computers allow the HOST to disconnect from the IMP, to cross-patch its end of the IMP cable, and to perform loop-back transmission tests, all under program control.

Because of the symmetry in IMP-HOST interface design, we can describe the 6-wire transmission scheme from "sender" to "receiver", ignoring which is the IMP and which is the HOST <BBN1822>. The six signals are (1) receiver ready test, (2) receiver master ready, (3) sender data, (4) sender last bit, (5) sender bit ready, and (6) receiver ready for next bit.

Two of the 6 wires are used by the sender to determine whether the receiver is operational. The sender puts a signal (e.g., signal ground) on one of the pair ("receiver ready test") and interprets the return of that signal on the second of the pair ("receiver master ready") to mean that the receiver is in good health. The receiver confirms his good health by looping "receiver ready test" back through "receiver master ready" with a switch (e.g., a relay or transistor). When the receiver malfunctions, it is expected that some mechanism (e.g., a watch-dog timer) soon turns off the "master ready" loopback switch and thereby notifies the sender of the receiver's demise <Ornstein>. The latest specifications do not demand a HOST watch-dog timer, but rather ask that some discipline be adopted to insure that the HOST ready line is dropped when a HOST is to discontinue HOST-IMP message exchanges.

The remaining 4 of the 6 wires are used for bit-serial message transfer. In addition to a wire through which actual data bits flow, there are (1) two hand-shake wires for controlling asynchronous bit transfer and (2) a "last bit" indicator to mark the ends of bit-serial messages. The hand-shake works as follows.

Upon placing a data bit on the data line, the sender enters the "bit ready" state (the "bit ready" signal stays down for a moment) and waits for the receiver's "ready for next bit" signal to be high.

The receiver indicates his willingness to accept a data bit by raising the "ready for next bit" signal. He then waits for the returning "bit ready" signal to be high.

When the sender (in the "bit ready" state) sees that the receiver's "ready for next bit" signal is high, he raises his "bit ready" signal and waits for the "ready for next bit" signal to drop.

When the receiver sees the "bit ready" go high in response to his "ready for next bit", he takes the data bit from the "data" line and drops his "ready for next bit" signal (for some minimum time) as a "got it" indication.

When the sender sees the "ready for next bit" signal drop, he interprets that as a "got it" indication, and leaves "bit ready" state until a new data bit can be placed on the "data" line. And so on.

When placing the last bit of a message on the data line, the sender raises the "last bit" signal for appropriate interpretation by the receiver.

See BBN's IMP-HOST interface manual <BBN1822> for a more detailed description of the hand-shake mechanism and of the schematic in Figure 7-2.

Using this simple hand-shake protocol, it is possible for either the sender or receiver to suspend transmission indefinitely, bit by bit, without losing data. Transfers can thereby proceed at the maximum rate allowed by the slower end (as a function of time).

As of this writing, the IMPs are set to limit data transfers to a maximum of 100 Kbps (10 microseconds per bit) so as to conserve on total IMP bandwidth (available processor cycles per second). While hardware interfaces can operate into the Mbps (megabits per second) range, HOSTs often limit data transfer themselves from time to time under varying system load.

At various times during their connection, a HOST and an IMP will each have occasion to slow the flow of data from the other; a HOST may find itself busy with some device when some IMP data becomes available and, similarly, an IMP may find its buffers momentarily full when some HOST data becomes available. The asynchronous bit-by-bit IMP-HOST handshake provides a very fine-grained mechanism by which a receiver can control the flow of data so as to meet its processing requirements. This is our first example of a so-called "flow control" mechanism; the problem of flow control appears often in communication and particularly in our consideration of packet techniques in computer communication.

The scheme used in the IMP-HOST interface generalizes to a 5+P wire system (P=1 in the IMP-HOST system) in which there are P data lines (P for "Packet") operated under the same hand-shake mechanism.

Assume we are given that the signal propagation delay between sender and

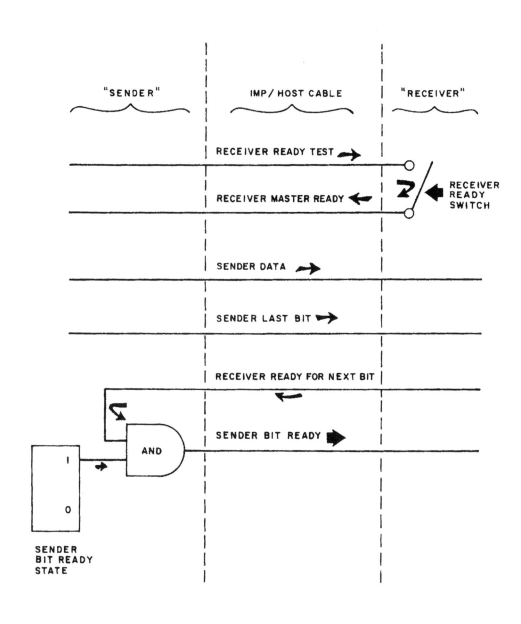

FIGURE 7-2 IMP-HOST "SENDER" AND "RECEIVER" SIGNALS

116

receiver is D seconds (D is calculated from cable length in feet divided by signal speed in feet per second). It takes a minimum, say, of Ws seconds and Wr seconds for the sender and receiver to generate and dispense with P data bits, respectively. We now calculate the maximum data-rate C (for "Capacity" in bits per second) of the hand-shake procedure by looking at the minimum time between rising edges of "sender bit ready" at the sender.

"Sender bit ready" can only go high if both (1) the sender is in the "bit ready state" and (2) the "receiver ready for next bit" is high at the sender end. It takes D seconds for the rising edge of the "sender bit ready" signal to propagate to the receiver, during which nothing else happens. Assuming that the receiver drops his "ready for next bit" line instantly after he sees the "sender bit ready" signal go high, we observe that two partially overlapped periods must pass before the "sender bit ready" signal comes high again. The first of these is the period required (1) for the sender to see the "ready for next bit" signal drop as a "got it" indicator (D seconds) and (2) for him to produce a new data bit (Ws seconds), totaling D+Ws seconds. The second period is that required (1) for the receiver to dispense with the newly received data bit (Wr seconds) and (2) for his new "ready for next bit" signal to be seen high at the sender (D seconds), totaling Wr+D seconds. The "sender bit ready" signal goes high again only after both periods have passed, only after a number of seconds equal to the maximum of the two. So that:

(Eq 7-1)
$$C = \frac{P}{2D + \max(Ws, Wr)}$$

For an ARPANET IMP-HOST interface with P=1 data wire, D=60 nanoseconds (30 feet at, say, 2 nanoseconds per foot), and with Wr≤Ws=10 microseconds, we get that the maximum bit-rate is about 100 Kbps. At 2000 feet the maximum bit-rate is about 55 Kbps. If this scheme were used at a mile, the maximum effective bit-rate would be down to about 33 Kbps.

Be sure to note that the hand-shake used for flow control between a HOST and its IMP makes channel capacity depend on delay; this dependence is found again and again in the ARPANET. As we see in our analysis of store-and-forward packet communication in the report proper, the interdependence of capacity and delay resulting from flow control is fundamental to computer communication.

To increase the maximum IMP-HOST bit-rate, the IMP delay of 10 microseconds (i.e., Ws or Wr) can be adjusted down <BBN1822>. At long distances and/or much higher data rates, the required errorlessness of transmission is easily challenged.

Another approach one might use to improve the bit-rate would be to add data wires (P>1) for "byte-serial" asynchronous transmission. The above bit-serial scheme is used between IMP and HOST because (1) the data-rates acceptable to an IMP are not much higher than that possible via the serial exchange, (2) it is not anticipated that HOSTs be far from IMPs, (3) HOST processing power and transmission rates vary widely from HOST to HOST and from time to time, and (4) the bit stream approach avoids any word-length biases in an environment with many different computers and word lengths (e.g., 16, 24, 32, 36, 60, and 128 bits per word). While the ARPANET currently uses the bit as its atomic unit of transfer, it has been found that the resulting generality is too much of a burden and that the 8-bit byte (say) might be a better choice (i.e., P=8) < McKenzie2>.

IMP-HOST Protocol

With IMP-HOST interface hardware between them, an IMP and a HOST become capable of exchanging messages of an arbitrary length (in bits). IMP-HOST Protocol <BBN1822> establishes the convention that all legal messages between a HOST and its IMP include a 32 bit header and be of maximum length 8095 bits. There are a number of message types which can go between a HOST and its IMP. The two most important kinds of message are the "regular" data message and the "ready for next message" (RFNM) message.

A regular IMP-HOST message has an 8-bit HOST identifier and an 8-bit LINK identifier. When going from HOST to IMP, a regular message is a request on the IMP Subnet to deliver the contained bits to the specified HOST with the specified LINK identifier. When going from IMP to HOST, a regular message contains bits sent by the specified HOST with the specified LINK identifier.

A RFNM is a 32 bit control message which comes to a HOST from its IMP as an acknowledgment of the arrival of a previously sent regular message, at the specified remote HOST, with the specified LINK identifier. Each HOST sees a set of 256 communication LINKs to each of 256 possible HOSTs. For each regular message sent to a specified HOST on a specified LINK, a HOST can expect to receive a RFNM containing that HOST/LINK identification after the remote destination IMP has begun transferring the message to the remote HOST.

If one thinks of LINKs as wires, a RFNM acknowledges the arrival of a message at the other end of a HOST-HOST wire. It is guaranteed by the IMP Subnet that messages sent to a HOST on a given LINK will arrive in the order sent.

A basic problem for the IMP Subnet is to control the generation of messages so as to match the capacity of the IMPs and the computing power of communicating HOST processes. We distinguish between <u>flow control</u> and <u>congestion control</u>. Flow control mechanisms are those which prevent a sender from swamping a receiver with more data than it can process or store. Congestion control mechanisms are those which insure equitable access to communications facilities among populations of senders and receivers.

A RFNM is a message generated by a "destination" <u>IMP</u>. The RFNM was originally used as a congestion control mechanism in that (as of <BBN1822>, April 1972) it was a detectable violation of IMP-HOST Protocol to send a message to a given HOST on a given LINK until that given HOST/LINK "wire" had been unblocked by the receipt of a RFNM for the previous message. LINK blocking via RFNM control was intended to keep HOSTs from clogging the IMP Subnet by choking them off from further transmission until previous messages have left the Subnet.

A simple calculation reveals that the LINK mechanism for IMP Subnet congestion control is not sufficient. An IMP is a Honeywell DDP-516 or DDP-316 with 12,000 16-bit core memory words of which more than half are used to hold the IMP program. An IMP has room for on the order of 100,000 bits of buffered data. The virtual storage capacity of the IMP Subnet between two specified HOSTs (implied by the LINK mechanism) is on the order of 2,000,000 bits (i.e., 8095 bits per message, times 256 LINKs per HOST, times 1 outstanding message per LINK). If a destination HOST were to be accepting data at a rate less than that of a sending HOST and if the sending HOST were to use all the LINKs available to it, then the total number of bits in the Subnet in support of this one HOST-HOST communication could grow to be enough to fill more than 20 IMPs.

This obvious calculation has been performed on countless occasions and its validity supported by actual ARPANET lock-ups <Frank1>. A new congestion control scheme has already been invented by BBN. The number of "effective LINKs" is reduced to 4. While RFNMs are still returned as before, they have significance only in that they are required to keep compatibility with existing HOST-HOST software. Congestion due to slow destination HOSTs is limited by blocking the communications of over-ambitious sending HOSTs. Under the new scheme, long messages (i.e., those over a 1000 bits) are delayed at their source until a verified allocation of space is made for them at the destination IMP. The overriding objective of such IMP-HOST congestion control mechanisms is to keep the Communications Subnet empty so that small messages from carefully managed sending HOSTs can move quickly to highly receptive receiving HOSTs <McQuillan>.

IMP-IMP Protocol: A Scenario

We now follow the movement of a particular message from a "sending" HOST to a "receiving" HOST through the IMP Subnet to sketch the workings of IMP-IMP Protocol. We start with a cold "sending" HOST. The IMP connected to this cold "sending" HOST believes that the HOST is disconnected from the ARPANET because the "HOST ready test" signal through the IMP-HOST interface is not being returned through the "HOST master ready" line of the 12 wire cable. Knowledge of the disconnectedness of the "sending" HOST propagates with other status data among the IMPs every 1/2 second and so all IMPs know that the "sending" HOST is down with respect to the ARPANET. Any messages marked for routing to our "sending" HOST (1) are intercepted at their point of Subnet entry, (2) are discarded, and (3) are reported so to their source HOST.

Suddenly, the IMP attached to our "sending" HOST notices that our "sending" HOST's "HOST master ready" signal has come on and prepares itself for a possible message exchange. This start up event is not expected to happen often, certainly not for each message, and so the IMP-HOST protocol for handling it is allowed to be relatively elaborate to serve a number of purposes.

In preparation for sending the one 8095 bit data message we are following through the IMP Subnet, the "sending" HOST must bring itself from the starting cold state into a state of ongoing communication with its IMP; a state, incidentally, in which it would like to remain for hours, days, or even weeks, if possible. It does so (1) by turning on its "HOST ready indicator" thereby looping back the IMP's "HOST ready test" signal and (2) by sending a few IMP-HOST no-op messages to its IMP as proof of its willingness to communicate.

The IMP responds to these new signs of life by sending a few gratuitous

IMP-HOST no-op messages of its own to the "sending" HOST to establish the viability of the IMP-to-HOST connection. The IMP then suspends communication for some number of tens of seconds to allow information about the "sending" HOST's availability to propagate via the 1/2 second IMP-IMP status exchanges to the far reaches of the IMP Subnet. When all IMPs have had time to learn of our "sending" HOST's change in status, the IMP connected to the "sending" HOST is then prepared to route messages to and from it. This start-up message exchange and delay is experienced only when a HOST first comes up on the ARPANET (e.g., daily). Thereafter, the IMP Subnet remains aware of the HOST's availability and the tens of seconds delay is not encountered.

In our scenario it is the "sending" HOST's desire to transmit data to a specified "receiving" HOST which leads to the next event of note. Having collected (1) up to 8063 bits of data, (2) an 8 bit HOST identifier, and (3) an 8 bit LINK identifier, all from sources outside this discussion (according to some HOST-HOST protocol), the "sending" HOST initiates a transfer as a regular HOST-to-IMP data message through the IMP-HOST interface. Note that there are 16 additional bits in a HOST-to-IMP leader which bring the maximum total up to 8095 bits <BBN1822>. At the hardware level, the transfer proceeds a bit at a time according to the previously discussed asynchronous hand-shake hardware protocol and message bits find their way into the IMP core memory.

After the 1000th bit of the at most 8095 bit message enters the IMP's core, the IMP picks up the 1000 bits with its destination HOST/LINK pair and, noting (say) that the specified HOST is actively communicating, creates a packet which it immediately turns over to its store-and-forward module for routing to the specified destination. With the "sending" HOST's message only partially received, its IMP has already started the initial packet toward its destination from IMP to IMP over appropriate telephone circuits. Note that (as indicated) the words "message" and "packet" have particular technical meanings in Subnet terminology: messages are up to about 8095 bits long and are exchanged by HOSTs, while packets are up to about 1000 bits long and are exchanged by IMPs.

At this point, the IMP has forwarded the first packet of our (up to) 8095 bit message and waits for a response from the destination IMP telling it that there is space for message reassembly. Then, as the message continues to flow into IMP core from the "sending" HOST (at about 100 Kbps maximum, depending on HOST processing) subsequent 1000 bit packets are collected, labelled, and turned over for routing. Finally, the last message bit (as indicated by the IMP-HOST interface "HOST last bit" signal) leaves the "sending" HOST, enters IMP core, is placed in the last (≤8th) IMP packet, and begins its journey through the IMP system toward the "receiving" HOST.

The "sending" HOST, having transferred the last bit of the message in question, notes that it should expect to get a RFNM message for the specified "receiving" HOST/LINK pair at some later time. According to the old IMP-HOST protocol and to standard practice among HOSTs even today, the HOST/LINK pair is "blocked" until the corresponding RFNM is returned. The "sending" HOST goes on either to send messages on other, unblocked LINKs or to compute in some other context. In our scenario, the next interesting event to involve the "sending" HOST will be the arrival of said RFNM.

The message we are following from "sending" HOST to "receiving" HOST is now in the Communications Subnet in the form of some number of 1000 bit packets each marked with its destination HOST/LINK pair and its position in the HOST-HOST message. Note again that messages flow (virtually) among HOSTs and packets (really) among IMPs. The IMP Subnet has accepted responsibility for the successful error-free transmission of our message to the "receiving" HOST. This responsibility now rides with each of the up to 8 packets as they wind their way separately from IMP to IMP.

The first decision an IMP must make about a packet which it holds is where to send it, i.e., how to advance its routing toward the specified destination. If the packet is designated for receipt by a HOST connected to the current IMP, the packet is handed by the IMP's store-and-forward module to its message preparation module. If the packet is to be routed to some HOST connected to a remote IMP, then the holding IMP must decide through which telephone circuit (which leg) to put the packet so as to optimize its path toward the destination. This is the routing decision.

To provide inputs for routing decisions, an IMP maintains a dynamically updated table of destination delays which indicates which next leg will minimize the transit time of a packet to its destination. The table is updated via the 1/2 second IMP-IMP status exchanges. Routing data is generated by a local exchange of data, i.e., an exchange among immediate neighbors. Each IMP maintains a table of transit times (by destination) which it updates on the basis of its own modem queues and the times received from its neighbors <Heart>.

The maintenance of the set of routing tables across the Subnet constitutes an asynchronously iterated distributed computation. IMPs have no prior knowledge of global ARPANET topology, but rather maintain an evolving data base to help in a local optimization of packet routing.

IMP's direct packets through the Subnet so as to minimize transit time. It is likely that the optimal next leg toward a given destination will change with traffic and circuit availability. In particular, packets of the same message will often take different paths to a destination, due especially to their own collisions. Each IMP routes packets so as to minimize transit time; it would not be unusual for packets going to some single destination to leave an IMP through different circuits -- over circuits other than those with long queues of earlier arriving packets to the same destination.

Having been placed on a queue for a given circuit, a packet gets transmitted through some modem interface. As it goes out on the line, the modem hardware generates synchronization characters (SYNCHs), data, and a 24 bit cyclic checksum. The receiving IMP's modem interface moves the data into IMP memory while computing its check sum and notifies the receiving IMP whether the packet has been damaged in transmission. If the packet has been damaged, it is immediately discarded. If there are no buffers available for subsequent packets, the newly arrived packet is discarded <Zeigler>. If the packet is error-free and additional buffers are available, the packet is formally accepted by the new (receiving) IMP and an acknowledgement is returned to the sending IMP. If either the packet or its acknowledgment are damaged or lost in transmission or if the packet is rejected due to insufficient storage, the sending IMP will fail to get a successful acknowledgment and will retransmit the packet after some time-out period.

During all of this, the IMP is paying strict attention to the performance characteristics of its circuits so that if a circuit starts damaging too many packet transmissions, the routing module will direct packets down alternative legs. A message exchange routine is constantly maintained between IMPs joined by a circuit so that each of the IMPs can assess the quality of the circuit. This exchange continues even after a circuit has been declared dead so that when a circuit recovers, it is automatically put back into service.

An interesting sidelight of continuing IMP surveillance of telephone circuit performance is that it would not be difficult for the IMP system to produce a trouble report for the telephone company something like: "On May 31, 1972, at 12:01:32.768 hours, circuit number 'NW-123-456' went 'down' for l00 milliseconds. Please see to it that this doesn't happen again".

After an appropriate number of routings and retransmissions, the packets of our message begin to arrive at the destination IMP where they are handed over to the message preparation module. The packets arrive at the destination IMP in no particular order, since each has percolated through the IMP Subnet independently of the others, subject to varying routing decisions and error-correcting retransmissions. As the packets arrive they are reassembled into a HOST message and, when all have been accounted for, the message is queued up for transmission via a IMP-HOST interface into the "receiving" HOST.

As the first packet of the message enters the HOST, the destination IMP constructs a RFNM message (i.e., a "ready for next message" message) which is then routed back as a single packet message to the "sending" HOST. The RFNM propagates in exactly the same way as a single packet data message, except that a RFNM does not generate a RFNM at its destination IMP.

As the last packet of our data message enters the "receiving" HOST, the "IMP last bit" signal is raised. The "receiving" HOST examines the newly completed message's IMP-HOST header to discover that it has received data from the HOST on the LINK therein specified. Concurrently the "sending" HOST receives a RFNM as an acknowledgment of message receipt and unblocks the given HOST/LINK pair for subsequent transmission.

IMP-IMP Protocol: Observations

We make three observations about IMP-HOST and IMP-IMP protocol as just sketched: (1) that the time required for all of these machinations by HOSTs and IMPs is well within the tolerances of interactive computer networking, (2) that the transmission error control supplied by the Subnet is of sufficiently high quality that other sources of error must now be confronted, and (3) that an interesting deadlock may exist between the technique of message disassembly and possibilities in the development of follow-on IMPs.

Time required. Early specifications for the ARPANET called for a maximum propagation delay time between any two nodes of under .5 seconds <Roberts>. That specification has been met and with such success that the time-sharing systems being used over the ARPANET are themselves the limiting factors in their own interactive use. The DDP-516's and DDP-316's being used as IMPs have already been far surpassed in speed and low cost by many newer products in the minicomputer market (e.g., PDP-11 and NOVA). Communications circuits of significantly higher bandwidths (e.g., much greater than 230.4 Kbps) at lower cost are imminent. Therefore, the potential for economic application of ARPANET techniques is even greater than that demonstrated in the IMP Subnet.

Error control. Experience with the ARPANET has shown that the error rates in telephone circuits (quoted as 1 bit in error out of 100,000 bits) have not been a significant factor in limiting ARPANET performance <Kahn2, Ornstein>. The IMP modem interfaces generate a 24 bit cyclic checksum per (up to) 1000 bit packet to reduce the undetected transmission error rate to one bit in ten to the twelfth bits or about one undetected ARPANET transmission bit error per year <Roberts>. The fact that there have been enough bits in error in the ARPANET to fill this quota for centuries, leads us to look at the newly dominant error sources.

In the IMP Subnet itself, there are two major trouble spots for error control. The first, and most obvious, is that there is no error checking done across the IMP-HOST interface. It is a fact that these interfaces have been generating errors and it is interesting to note that no higher level protocols (e.g., HOST-HOST, File Transfer) have been developed which check for end-to-end integrity of transmitted data. A more dangerous source of errors in the ARPANET are the core memories of the IMP's themselves. IMP core memories (1) are not parity checked, (2) are prone to failure (to wit, a DDP-516 "jump to self" instruction reputedly overheats core memory causing bits to be dropped), and (3) are not rigorously error-checked by the IMP program (i.e., packet checksums exist only "on the wires"). If a bit in some buffer of some IMP somewhere were to malfunction (even solidly) the error would be intermittent to the extent that packet routing is load dependent and that packets will fall in various buffers on repeated passage through the same IMP. It is reassuring to note that recent versions of the IMP program have included core-to-core, software, packet checksums, especially on routing information, to detect, correct, and even report many IMP core failures.

Because error detection has been missing in HOST-HOST communication protocols, there are few (if any) real statistics on the magnitude of the error problem. Because the IMP Subnet is advertised as being error-free (transmission error-free), protocol designers (e.g., we) have thus far avoided higher level error control and left themselves exposed.

Message disassembly. The most famous and well-understood bug in the initial implementation of the ARPANET Communications Subnet is the "reassembly lock-up problem" <Frank1>. This bug is "fixed" in the current implementation by the previously mentioned use of IMP-IMP allocation protocol for multi-packet messages <McQuillan>.

Under the initial implementation, two HOSTs begin a massive data transfer utilizing full 8095 bit multi-packet messages and multiple LINKs for high data-rates. As the number of LINKs is increased past some small number like 3 or 4, the total throughput not only stops increasing, but suddenly drops off until at some slightly larger number of LINKs the entire ARPANET locks up, i.e., requires manual intervention to get data flowing again.

The cause of reassembly lock-up, with benefit of considerable hindsight, is easy to identify. By using multiple LINKs, a sending HOST can get more than 1 or 2 multi-packet messages in the IMP Subnet at once. Say that the sender is so successful that he gets at least one more message into the Subnet than there is room to hold in reassembly buffers at the destination IMP. Also say that due to vagaries in routing and retransmission, at least one packet of each of these messages gets into the reassembly buffers at the destination IMP just as the reassembly buffer pool is exhausted. Lock-up is then achieved. There is no room for the additional packets required to complete the partially assembled messages in the destination IMP and so all packets sent to that IMP are discarded. Because the IMP Subnet takes its responsibility for message integrity very seriously, thoughts of automatically junking packets in this lock-up situation are inadmissable. The sending HOST continues to flood the Subnet until IMP buffers are full throughout the ARPANET, IMPs are transmitting in many directions at full speed, and most transmissions are being discarded due to insufficient storage <Zeigler>.

The situation is remarkably like the deadlock which arises when there are two magnetic tape drives available on an operating system and two two-drive programs are each assigned only one.

The new IMP system has been installed with a relatively complex allocation scheme whereby multi-packet messages are only permitted into the Subnet after an acknowledged allocation of space has been made at the destination IMP. A less sophisticated observer (e.g., we) would suggest that the problem of reassembly could be solved by eliminating disassembly, i.e., by eliminating multi-packet messages. It can be argued that the simplicity resulting from removing disassembly and reassembly would more than repay the alleged loss of performance. But the argument is more subtle and more interesting than one might expect.

The IMPs do disassembly for a number of reasons. The original ARPANET specifications called for 8095 bit messages. Transmission efficiency under burst-errors and the utilization of IMP memory for fixed-length blocks are both thought to be optimized by packet sizes on the order of 1000 bits. By using 1000 bit packets, large multi-packet messages can be pipe-lined through the Subnet, the first packet being sent on its way before the second has even entered the source IMP. By using 1000 bit packets, a message can be propagated in parallel through the ARPANET's redundant telephone circuits to achieve bit-rates in excess of that of any one circuit. Finally, if the message size were smaller, say equal to that of a packet, then the overhead incurred by HOST computers in handling messages would be increased.

But now the interesting deadlock. Because the IMPs are constructed with general purpose computers, processor bandwidth limitations are such that the pipe-lining effect of disassembly significantly reduces delay and improves throughput for multi-packet messages. Because the IMP program is becoming increasingly complex owing to the inherent difficulties of disassembly and the allocation schemes which deal with them, the IMP can only be (as it is) effectively implemented in software on a general purpose computer.

By simplifying IMP operations (e.g., by removing disassembly), follow-on IMPs can be built for high performance nearly all in "hardware", whereupon the overall performance will be so improved as to swamp any gains attributable to disassembly.

We look with great excitement to BBN's recent work on a high-speed modular IMP which promises to answer the question we raise and many others <Heart1>.

Appendix B
ARPANET HOST-HOST Protocol

A typical HOST has an existence apart from the ARPANET; many HOSTs even predate the IMP Subnet, some by as much as five years. The Subnet does nothing more than bring to the HOSTs, as described in the preceding appendix, a way to quickly and inexpensively send messages to each other. Like the League of Nations before it, the ARPANET brings to its members an opportunity to escape isolation, to cooperate toward common ends.

Before HOSTs can cooperate via the IMP Subnet, they need to agree on the rendezvous, format, and timing of messages to be exchanged -- they must have a protocol. Any such set of agreements between or among HOSTs is called "a HOST-HOST protocol". There have been many HOST-HOST protocols in the short history of the ARPANET: one to connect a computer terminal on a certain HOST to a certain "JOB" on another certain HOST, one to send an ASCII file from a certain disk in Salt Lake City to a disk in Menlo Park, and one to copy records from a magnetic tape in Oklahoma to another in California, for example. But, as you might infer from these examples, the various HOST-HOST protocols led to a great deal of duplicated effort and inconvenience as each application required the specific HOSTs involved to come to new agreements and new implementations. And so one HOST-HOST protocol, called "the official HOST-HOST Protocol", was developed to provide a set of general communication procedures for use by various HOSTs in various applications.

In the preceding appendix we looked out into the IMP Subnet; we now turn to look back, inside the HOSTs, to survey the structures which evolved within these pre-existing computing systems to deal with the problems of protocol in a packet communication network. We discuss several special-purpose

HOST-HOST protocols, mainly to give some historical context, and then move on to sketch the operation of the "official" general-purpose HOST-HOST protocol. With some observations about protocol design, we leave you to our theories of interprocess communication in the report proper and to the detailed literature <Carr, Crocker, Newkirk, McKenzie1, Bhushan4, Bhushan5, Bressler, McKenzie2, Burchfiel, Kalin1>.

Other HOST-HOST Protocols

Prior to the invention of the "official" ARPANET HOST-HOST Protocols, a number of protocols were invented either (1) to develop confidence in basic ARPANET hardware and software, or (2) to fill an immediate need for intercomputer communication.

Our experiences with special-purpose HOST-HOST protocols were purely experimental. Three protocols were developed in early 1970 involving the MIT Project MAC DMCG PDP-10 in cooperation with, respectively, (1) MIT Multics, (2) the Harvard PDP-10, and (3) a combination of the Harvard PDP-10, the Harvard PDP-1, and the Project MAC Evans and Sutherland LDS-1 (picture processor).

The first protocol effort made it possible, under special arrangement, to make one IMLAC console on a dedicated PDP-10 behave something like a Multics terminal via the ARPANET <Padlipsky>. The second Protocol made it possible to make that same IMLAC into a terminal on Harvard's PDP-10. Both of these experiments were well worth the effort, not in their end product, but rather in their use as tools in developing ARPANET expertise and in exposing problems in terminal interfacing <Metcalfe>.

Our (with Barker and Cohen at Harvard) third experimental HOST-HOST protocol was more ambitious in that it involved four major processors, three of which were joined only by the ARPANET. A PDP-10/LDS-1 display program of considerable complexity (i.e., Cohen's Aircraft Carrier Landing Program) was edited and assembled on Harvard's PDP-10; it was transmitted to MIT's PDP-10/LDS-1; and the dynamically changing picture it generated was then transmitted via the ARPANET back to Harvard's PDP-1 to be displayed. The results of this experiment expose some additional lessons in the coordination of remote processes and verification of the fact that the ARPANET supplies insufficient bandwidth for brute-force dynamic graphics <Metcalfe>.

In parallel, at least two other HOST-HOST communication efforts were performed. Between the Stanford Research Institute (SRI) and the University of Utah, a protocol was established to permit SRI people to do program development on Utah's PDP-10 in preparation for their move from an SDS-940 to a PDP-10.

Taft, Barker, and Sundberg developed a protocol at Harvard by which their PDP-1 with its four DEC scopes becomes a very fancy terminal for the Harvard PDP-10 over the ARPANET. This experiment was an early attempt at terminal support through the ARPANET, later followed by Conrad's PDP-1 Monitor at Harvard, BBN's TIP <Ornstein, Mimno> and the University of Illinois's ARPANET terminal-support system. Two HOSTs, namely Tinker and McClellan Air Force Base's UNIVAC 418's, were used strictly for magnetic tape file transfer. Their HOST-HOST protocol ignored all other HOSTs and was optimized for efficient use in routine tape transfer.

While most of these protocols (and the programs written to support them) have fallen into disuse, some ad hoc HOST-HOST protocols persist and others will follow. The option to invent special HOST-HOST protocols, despite the existence of a general purpose HOST-HOST protocol, remains in the ARPANET to allow experimentation with new ideas in HOST-HOST communication and to support special applications requiring very high efficiency; this option is preserved in planning for a commercial version of the ARPANET <PCI>.

General Purpose NCP Protocols

The ARPANET IMP Subnet provides communication paths among HOSTs; the basic unit of activity in the ARPANET is not the HOST, however, but rather the user process or JOB. There are typically a large number of JOBs running concurrently on any given HOST at any given time. It was clear to early ARPANET designers that a HOST-HOST protocol would be required to multiplex the ARPANET's communications facilities among user processes on HOSTs, or rather, to create a virtual process-process (i.e., JOB-JOB) communications network <Roberts>.

After a long period of controversy, two general-purpose HOST-HOST protocols were forwarded. The first to be formally presented <Crocker1> (and later adopted by the ARPANET Network Working Group) is oriented around a system of "connections"; we call it "the NCP protocol" from "Network Control

Program". The second to be formally presented <Walden> (and the one currently being studied as a sideline in ARPANET development <Bressler1>) is oriented around a system of process-process "messages"; we call it "the MSP protocol" from "Message Switching Protocol".

The connection-oriented NCP protocol adopted by the ARPANET Network Working Group is an extension of the LINK mechanism of the IMP Subnet. Establishing a process-process (i.e., JOB-JOB) connection is essentially the assignment of a HOST-HOST LINK to a process port (SOCKET) pair <Bhushan3, McKenzie1>. The basic transactions among so-called "Network Control Programs" (NCPs) obeying the HOST-HOST protocol are simply those of (1) requesting that a LINK be allocated to a certain process-process (i.e., SOCKET-SOCKET) simplex data path, (2) routing a byte stream from a connection's send SOCKET to its receive SOCKET, (3) controlling the flow of data through a LINK so as to avoid swamping a receiving process, (4) interrupting communication over a connection for the handling of abnormal conditions, and (5) closing a connection and freeing its LINK.

The message-oriented MSP protocol currently being studied by Bressler and Walden preserves the message exchange texture of the IMP Subnet for the virtual, user-level interprocess communication system. Because an NCP for such a HOST-HOST protocol would do little more than multiplexing the use of the IMP-HOST interface, it could be simple and efficient. Because "connections" will no doubt be useful objects at some higher level of data exchange, the message-oriented NCP protocol passes more communications-oriented functions to higher level protocols and programs. Whether a "connection-oriented" NCP is more or less effective than a "message-oriented" NCP remains an open question <Bressler1>.

A Scenario for The NCP Protocol

The transmission of a byte-stream from one ARPANET user process to another goes something like the following. One of the processes (either the sending process or the receiving process) indicates to his local supervisor (his NCP therein) that he wishes to be receptive to requests for connection to a specified socket. His use of a specific 32-bit SOCKET number may be access-controlled to any extent desired by the local system <Bhushan3>. Whether his request to be receptive is at all selective is another option which might be exercised. In this case the supervisor registers the process's receptivity by making an entry in a local "SOCKET table". The process is said to be "listening" for a request for connection on the specified SOCKET.

Elsewhere in the network, the other process (called the "initiating" process) indicates to his supervisor that he wishes to request a (simplex) connection between his specified local SOCKET and a specified remote SOCKET at a remote HOST. On his behalf, the NCP sends a HOST-HOST control message (i.e., a "Request For Connection" (RFC) to the specified HOST and registers this fact by making an entry in its local SOCKET table. The initiating process is said to have a SOCKET in "RFC sent" state.

At this point we have (1) a listening SOCKET, (2) an initiating SOCKET, and (3) a "request for connection" HOST-HOST control message in transit between them.

At some later time (within .5 seconds) the RFC arrives at its destination where the NCP notices that the target SOCKET specified in the RFC matches an active entry in its SOCKET table and that the connection can be completed. The listening process is notified of the RFC's arrival and an answering RFC message is sent back to the initiating HOST. With the arrival of the answering RFC, the initiating NCP marks the connection "open" and notifies the initiating process.

In the RFC exchange leading to a successful connection, a HOST-HOST LINK is specified. The LINK is allocated to the new connection by whichever is to be the "receiving" NCP. Note that a SOCKET can be either on the "listening" or "initiating" end of a process-process simplex connection and, independently, can be either "receiving" or "sending" data through it.

At this point one would expect data to begin flowing from sender to receiver, but one additional kind of message exchange is required. The flow of data through a connection is controlled by the receiver via HOST-HOST allocation control messages. Before any data can flow, a sender must have received a permission (i.e., an allocation) to send a specified number of bytes in a specified number of messages.

This limiting of data flow by a receiver is intended to handle buffering and processing mismatches between computer systems of varying capability.

The receiving NCP with the now "open" connection next sends an allocation message (also a HOST-HOST control message) to the specified sending NCP. An accounting is maintained of outstanding allocations. The size of allocations is a function of the size of buffers between the receiving HOST's NCP and the receiving process. As data flows from sender to receiver, the sender's allocation is depleted and, as new allocation messages arrive, it is augmented <McKenzie1>.

Data is handed to the sending NCP by the sending process in some HOST-specific manner (a JOB-NCP protocol) with a specified local SOCKET. Using the specified SOCKET, (1) a destination HOST and LINK are retrieved from the local SOCKET table, (2) the allocation is checked and appropriately decremented, and (3) the data is sent. Data messages arriving at the receiving HOST are identified as to sending HOST and LINK and are routed to the appropriate receiving process with information retrieved from the locally maintained SOCKET table.

A connection can be closed from either end. The closing process indicates (e.g., by a system call) to his local NCP that he wishes to terminate a connection. The local NCP sends an appropriately tagged "close" HOST-HOST control message to the NCP at the other end of the connection. Upon receiving an echoing "close" from the remote NCP, the local NCP deletes any knowledge of the connection from its SOCKET table. An NCP receiving a "close" from the remote end of one of its open connections, notifies the owning process of connection termination and sends an echoing "close" as confirmation of the connection's removal from the SOCKET table.

Note that the above message exchanges support simplex (i.e., unidirectional) data flow only. If data is to flow in both directions between two user processes, two connections must be established and the above control transmissions duplicated for the reverse data flow.

HOST-HOST Protocol: Observations

We make four observations about the current connection-oriented HOST-HOST (NCP) protocol just sketched: (1) that it has been successful in providing a general purpose interprocess communication system for the ARPANET, (2) that the size and complexity of the required NCPs has been a significant factor in delaying ARPANET development, (3) that effective error control mechanisms are conspicuously absent, and (4) that there is evidence to suggest that ARPANET traffic will have a sufficiently large message-oriented component to justify message-oriented primitives at the NCP protocol level.

Success. Using the connection-oriented HOST-HOST protocol as a base, the ARPA community has successfully developed a (small) number of process-process protocols making substantive use of the ARPANET. LINK, SOCKET, connection and allocation have found acceptance as objects convenient for program manipulation in a wide variety of operating contexts (e.g., from PDP-10's to 360's).

Size and complexity. In establishing a connection, two remote processes (i.e., two NCP's) exchange messages toward the coordinated manipulation of remote data bases (i.e., SOCKET tables). For the connection system to function smoothly, care must be taken to maintain consistency in the various tables interlocked across the population of communicating HOSTs and user processes (i.e., JOBs). Each of the NCP's runs asynchronously with respect to the others and with respect to user processes in its own local system. The mechanisms required to manage the distributed body of state information supporting connections throughout the ARPANET are non-trivial, and connection-oriented NCPs are large and complex.

The size of NCP implementations alone (program, SOCKET tables, and system buffers) has been a significant deterrent to speedy implementation. Implementations with which we are familiar require on the order of 3000 words of supervisor space, not including tables and buffers; we recommend that you exercise care when making detailed probes in this delicate matter.

NCP complexity and concomitant difficulties of coding and debugging have been named as the principal cause of a six month schedule slip for ARPANET development. It is not that the complexity in managing connection-oriented communication can be avoided in any simple way, but that the assignment of this complexity to central supervisor level is a mistake. The relative scarcity of stand-alone time for supervisor debugging and the unmanageability of the internal supervisor environment are both significant.

Error control. We have already indicated that there is a potential error control problem in the IMP Subnet due to the fact that neither IMP core memories nor IMP-HOST interfaces are error-checked. It is also a fact that our complex connection-oriented NCP's drop bits, bytes, and even whole messages on occasion. Unfortunately, the NCP protocol, in all of its efforts to afford user processes a clean byte-stream communication system, has failed to treat error control. We have taken the IMP Subnet's guarantee of (transmission) error-free communication too much to heart (sic) and left ourselves exposed to the dangers of intermittent undetected error. There are some who claim that error control can and should be handled by higher level protocols <Bhushan1>. We agree, but hasten to add that our connection-oriented interface to these higher level protocols precludes any reasonable error recovery strategies. Indeed, this preclusion is manifest in the repeated avoidance of error control provisions in all higher level protocols to date, e.g., TELNET <O'Sullivan, O'Sullivan1, Postel>, and File Transfer <Bhushan6>.

The NCP protocol does not explicitly treat situations in which a HOST malfunction leads to a specific protocol violation or to a lack of response. HOST-HOST control messages which arrive in an improper context are often discarded and only occasionally logged. Many implementations treat a lack of response after some arbitrary time-out as a protocol violation and take punitive action against all the users on an offending HOST. Actions taken (1) usually lose information and/or cause catastrophic HOST-wide communications failures, (2) are non-standard, and (3) offer little potential for successful recovery <Burchfiel>.

Message-oriented traffic. Experience with the ARPANET has exposed several areas where critical interprocess communications are essentially message-oriented and therefore burdened significantly by the connection orientation of the current HOST-HOST protocol. The most notable of these is the Initial Connection Protocol (ICP) <Postel1> through which processes requiring a standard service find their way to an appropriate server. The ICP was the first "official" JOB-JOB protocol. The essence of an ICP is a message exchange whereby a using process submits a request for service to a standard address (published SOCKET number) and gets back a new address indicating where there is a process prepared to service that request. This simple exchange, which could be handled in two messages with a total of about 64 HOST-HOST data bits, requires, under the current HOST-HOST protocol, no fewer than 6 HOST-HOST messages (i.e., RFC, RFC, ALLOCATE, DATA, CLOSE, CLOSE) each with a minimum of 40 HOST-HOST header bits, not to mention the control information carefully entered and removed from two NCP SOCKET tables.

While the ICP is admittedly intended to be a relatively seldom-used communication function, the connection overhead for the simple message exchange is staggering and probably a forewarning of future difficulty. The construction of a connection-oriented NCP protocol is based on the assumption that, as a rule, most data exchanges will have extended duration. One should always be suspicious when one's first application of a rule generates an anomaly.

A second example of a mismatch between process-process message exchange and the connection-orientation of the current HOST-HCST protocol is found in the TELNET protocol. Whereas the HOST-HOST protocol goes to great lengths to allow NCP's to automate the buffering of data between sender and receiver, one of the more controversial facets of the TELNET protocol is that of providing a mechanism for draining NCP buffers which are, in general, an obstacle to interactive terminal use <Crocker>.

Bibliography

References to the Bibliography are tagged in the preceding text with (typically) the first author's name enclosed in angle brackets (e.g., <Author>). The references are alphabetized by first author's last name. Items marked with a NIC number have been archived by the ARPA Network Information Center ((415)329-0740) at the Stanford Research Institute's Augmentation Research Center in Menlo Park, California (94025). Items marked with an RFC number are included in a series of Requests for Comments maintained at the NIC by the ARPA Network Workinq Group (NWG). Items marked with an ASS number are included in the ARPANET Satellite System Notes at the NIC. Items marked with a PR number are included in the Packet Radio Temporary Notes at the NIC.

<Abramson>. N. Abramson, "The ALOHA system", University of Hawaii Technical Report Number B72-1, January 1972, also Computer Communication Networks, Prentice-Hall, 1972.

<Abramson1>. N. Abramson, "The ALOHA System", AFIPS Conference Proceedings, Volume 37, Page 281, Fall 1970.

<Abramson2>. N. Abramson, "Capacity and Excess Capacity of ALOHA Channels", presented at the Sixth Hawaii International Conference on System Sciences, January 1973, also ASS Notes #26 and #30, NIC #12735 and #13044, respectively.

<Abramson3>. N. Abramson, "ARPANET Satellite System", ASS Note #1, NIC #11283, March 1972.

<Abramson4>. N. Abramson, "ARPANET Satellite System", ASS Note #2, NIC #11284, March 1972.

<Abramson5>. N. Abramson, "ARPANET Satellite System", ASS Note #5, NIC #11287, May 1972.

<Abramson6>. N. Abramson, "ARPANET Satellite System", ASS Note #6, NIC #11288, May 1972.

<Abramson7>. N. Abramson, "Packet Switching with Satellites", AFIPS Conference proceedings, Volume 42, Page 695, June 1973.

<Akkoyunlu>. R. Akkoyunlu, A. Bernstein, R. Schantz, "An operating System for a Network Environment", Technical Report Number 5, Department of Computer Science, SUNY Stony Brook, March 1972.

<Anderson>. R. Anderson, V. Cerf, E. Harslem, J. Heafner, R. Metcalfe, et al., "The Data Reconfiguration Service -- An Experiment in Process/Process Communication", Proceedings of the Second Symposium on Problems in the Optimization of Data Communications Systems, Stanford University, October 1971, originally "Status Report on Proposed Data Reconfiguration Service", RFC #138, NIC #6715, April 1971, followed by "Data Reconfiguration Service -- An Implementation Specification", RFC #166, NIC #6780, and "The Data Reconfiguration Service -- Compiler/Interpreter", RFC #194, NIC #7100.

<Anderson1>. S.S. Anderson, "Graph Theory and Finite Combinatorics", Markham Publishing Company, 1970.

<Balzer>. R. M. Balzer, "PORTS -- A Method for Dynamic Inter-Program Communication and Job Control", AFIPS Conference Proceedings, May 1971.

<Balzer1>. R.M. Balzer, "Automatic Programming", Item 1, Institute Technical Memorandum, University of Southern California, Information Sciences Institute, September 1972.

<Balzer2>. R.M. Balzer, "An Overview of the ISPL Computer System Design", CACM, Volume 16, Number 2, February 1973.

<Baran>. P. Baran, et al., "On Distributed Communications", An 11 volume series of the RAND Corporation summarized in Volume 11, Memorandum RM-3767-PR, August 1964, NIC #6860.

<BBN1822>. "Specifications for the Interconnection of a HOST and an IMP", Bolt Beranek and Newman Inc., Report Number 1822, NIC #7958.

<Berger>. J.M. Berger, B. Mandelbrot, "A New Model for Error Clustering in Telephone Circuits", IBM Journal, Page 224, July 1963.

<Bhushan>. A.K. Bhushan, et al., "The Data Transfer Protocol", RFC #264, NIC #7812, November 1971.

<Bhushan1>. A.K. Bhushan, et al., "The File Transfer Protocol", RFC #265, NIC #7813, November 1971.

<Bhushan2>. A.K. Bhushan, "Another Look at Data and File Transfer Protocols", RFC #310, NIC #9261, April 1972.

<Bhushan3>. A.K. Bhushan, "Scenarios for Using ARPANET Computers", RFC #254, NIC #7695, October 1971.

<Bhushan4>. A. K. Bhushan, R. Metcalfe, J. Winett, "Socket Conventions Reconsidered", RFC #167, NIC #6784, May 1971.

<Bhushan5>. A. Bhushan, R. Kanodia, R. Metcalfe, J. Postel, "Comments on Byte Size for Connections", RFC #176, June 1971.

<Bhushan6>. A. Bhushan, "The File Transfer Protocol", RFC #354, NIC #10596, July 1972.

<Binder>. R. Binder, "Effects of Retransmission Delay on the Degradation of an ALOHA Channel", ASS Note #22, NIC #12166, November 1972.

<Binder1>. R. Binder, "Another ALOHA Satellite Protocol", presented at the Sixth Hawaii International Conference on System Sciences, January 1973, ASS Note #32, December 1972.

Bibliography

<Braden>. R. T. Braden, "Interim NETRJS Specifications", RFC #189, NIC #7133, July 1971.

<Braden1>. R.T. Braden, "NETRJS -- Remote Job Service Protocols for TIPs", RFC #283, NIC #8165, December 1971.

<Bressler>. R. D. Bressler, "Interprocess Communication on the ARPA Computer Network", MIT Civil Engineering, MS Thesis, May 1971.

<Bressler1>. B. Bressler, D. Murphy, D. Walden, "A Proposed Experiment with a Message Switching Protocol", RFC #333, NIC #9926, May 1972.

<Bressler2>. B. Bressler, R. Guida, A. McKenzie, "Remote Job Entry Protocol", NIC #12112.

<Brown>. G.W. Brown, J.G. Miller, T.A. Keenan, <u>EDUNET</u>, John Wiley & Sons, Inc., New York, 1967.

<Burchfiel>. J. Burchfiel, R. Tomlinson, "Proposed Change to Host-Host Protocol: Resynchronization of Connection Status", RFC #467, NIC #14741, February 1973.

<Buzen>. J.P. Buzen, "Queueing Network Models of Multiprogramming", Harvard PhD Thesis, August 1971.

<Carr>. C.S. Carr, S.D. Crocker, V.G. Cerf, "HOST-HOST Communications Protocol in the ARPA Network", AFIPS Conference Proceedings, May 1970.

<Cerf>. V.G. Cerf, "Formation of Network Measurement Group", RFC #323, NIC #9630, March 1972.

<Cerf1>. V. Cerf, "The Current Flow-Control Scheme for IMPSYS", RFC #442, NIC #13774, January 1973.

<Chang>. H.Y. Chang, "Hardware Maintainability and Software Reliability of Electronic Switching Systems", Proceedings of the 10th Allerton Conference on Circuits and Systems Theory, University of Illinois, October 1972.

<Cheatham>. T.E. Cheatham, "The Recent Evolution of Programming Languages", IFIPS Conference Proceedings, Ljubjana, Yugoslavia, August 23-28, 1971.

<Cheatham1>. T.E. Cheatham, B. Wegbreit, "A Laboratory for the Study of Automatic Programming", Report of the Center for Research in Computing Technology, Harvard University, November 1971.

<Chen>. T. C. Chen, "Distributed Intelligences", IBM Corporation, presented at the Sixth Hawaii International Conference on System Sciences, January 1973.

<Chu>. N.W. Chu, "A Study of Asynchronous Time Division Multiplexing for Time-Sharing Computer Systems", AFIPS Conference Proceedings, Volume 35, Page 669, Fall 1969.

<Cole>. G.D. Cole, "Computer Network Measurements: Techniques and Experiments", UCLA Computer Science Report Number UCLA-ENG-7165, October 1971.

<COMPCON73>. "Computing Networks from Minis through Maxis -- Are They for Real?", Digest of Papers, COMPCON73, IEEE Catalog Number 73CH0716-1C, Seventh Annual IEEE Computer Society International Conference, San Francisco, February 1973.

<Crocker>. S.D. Crocker, J.F. Heafner, R.M. Metcalfe, J.B. Postel, "Function-Oriented Protocols for the ARPA Computer Network", AFIPS Conference Proceedings, Volume 40, Page 271, May 1972.

<Crocker1>. S.D. Crocker, "HOST-HOST Protocol Document Number 1", NIC #5143, August 1970, obsoleted by <McKenzie1>.

<Crocker2>. S.D. Crocker, informal communication, May 1972.

<Crocker3>. S. Crocker, "Proposal for a Network Standard Format for a Data Stream to Control Graphics Display", RFC #86, NIC #5631, January 1971.

Bibliography

<Crowther>. W. Crowther, et al., "A System for Broadcast Communication: Reservation-ALOHA", Proceedings of the Sixth Hawaii International Conference on System Sciences, January 1973, also in more detail in ASS Note #23, November 1972.

<Datalanguage>. "Datalanguage", Datacomputer Project, Computer Corporation of America, Working Paper Number 3, October 1971.

<Davidson>. J. Davidson, "An Echoing Strategy for Satellite Links", University of Hawaii, RFC #357, NIC #10599, June 1972.

<Deutsch>. L.P. Deutsch, informal communication, January 1973.

<Directory>. "ARPA Network Current Directory of Network Participants", NIC #5150.

<Drake>. A.W. Drake, "Fundamentals of Applied Probability Theory", McGraw-Hill, 1967.

<Eastlake>. D. Eastlake, et al "ITS 1.5 Reference Manual", MIT Project MAC Artificial Intelligence Memo Number 161A, revised June 1968.

<ESS>. "No. 1 Electronic Switching System", The Bell System Technical Journal, Volume XLIII, Number 5, Parts 1 and 2, September 1964.

<Farber>. D.J. Farber, "Networks: An Introduction", DATAMATION, Volume 18, Number 4, April 1972.

<Feller>. W. Feller, "An Introduction to Probability Theory and its Applications", Volume I, Wiley, 1960, and Volume II, Wiley, 1966.

<Fisher>. D.A. Fisher, "Control Structures for Programming Languages", Carnegie-Mellon University, PhD Thesis, May 1970.

<Frank>. H. Frank, I.T. Frisch, W. Chou, "Topological Considerations in the Design of the ARPA Computer Network", AFIPS Conference Proceedings, May 1970.

Bibliography

<Frank1>. H. Frank, R.E. Kahn, L. Kleinrock, "Computer Communication Network Design -- Experience with Theory and Practice", AFIPS Conference Proceedings, Volume 40, Page 255, May 1972.

<Frank2>. H. Frank, R. Van Slyke, Network Analysis Corporation, informal talk on packet radio network design at SRI, December 1972, see <NAC>.

<Fultz>. G.L. Fultz, "Adaptive Routing Techniques for Message Switching Computer-Communication Networks", UCLA Computer Science Department, UCLA-ENG-7252, July 1972.

<Gaarder>. N.T. Gaarder, "ARPANET Satellite System", ASS Note #3, April 1972.

<Gorog>. E. Gorog, "Some New Classes of Cyclic Codes Used for Burst-Error Correction", IBM Journal, April 1963.

<Greenberger>. M. Greenberger, "Computers, Communications, and the Public Interest", The Johns Hopkins Press, Baltimore, 1971.

<Gruenberger>. F. Gruenberger, "Computers and Communications -- Toward a Computer Utility", Prentice-Hall Series in Automatic Computation, 1968.

<Habermann>. A. N. Habermann, "Synchronization of Communicating Processes", Communications of the ACM, Volume 15, Number 3, March 1972.

<Harslem>. E. Harslem, "Using Network Remote Job Entry", RFC #307, NIC #9258, February 1972.

<Harsleml>. E. Harslem, J. Heafner, "Some Thoughts on Network Graphics", RFC #94, NIC #5125, February 1971.

<Hayes>. J.F. Hayes, D.N. Sherman, "A Study of Data Multiplexing Techniques and Delay Performance", The Bell System Technical Journal, Volume 51, Number 9, November 1972.

Bibliography

<Heart>. F.E. Heart, R.E. Kahn, S.M. Ornstein, W.R. Crowther, D.C. Walden, "The Interface Message Processor for the ARPA Computer Network", AFIPS Conference Proceedings, Volume 36, Page 551, May 1970.

<Heart1>. F.E. Heart, S.M. Ornstein, W.R. Crowther, W.B. Barker, "A New Minicomputer-Multiprocessor for the ARPA Network", AFIPS Conference Proceedings, Volume 42, Page 529, June 1973.

<Heralds>. "Computer Networks: The Heralds of Resource Sharing", a movie written and directed by Steve King, first shown at the ICCC, October 1972.

<Hobgood>. W. S. Hobgood, "Evaluation of an Interactive-Batch System Marriage Reveals Ideal Mates", IBM Research, RC 3479, July 1971.

<Kahn>. R.E. Kahn, "Communications Principles for Operating Systems", internal memorandum at Bolt Beranek and Newman Inc., January 1972.

<Kahn1>. R.E. Kahn, "HOST Accounting and Administrative Procedures", RFC #136, NIC #6713, April 1971.

<Kahn2>. R.E. Kahn, informal communication, June 1972. See also Page 163 in Kahn's "Terminal Access to the ARPA Computer Network" in <Rustin>.

<Kahn3>. R.E. Kahn, W.R. Crowther, "A Study of ARPA Network Design and Performance", Report Number 2161, Bolt Beranek and Newman Inc., August 1971.

<Kahn4>. R.E. Kahn, W.R. Crowther, "Flow Control in a Resource Sharing Computer Network", Proceedings of the Second ACM IEEE Symposium on Problems in the Optimization of Data Communications Systems, Page 108, October 1971.

<Kalin>. R.B. Kalin, "Achieving Reliable Communication", RFC #203, NIC #7168, August 1971.

<Kalin1>. R.B. Kalin, "A Simplified NCP Protocol", RFC #60, NIC #4762, July 1970.

<Kalin2>. R.B. Kalin, "The Synthesis of Large Systems", PhD Thesis in preparation, Harvard University, 1973.

<Karp>. P.M. Karp, "Guide to Network Working Group Requests for Comments", NIC #5819, March 1971.

<Karp1>. P.M. Karp, "Origin, Development and Current Status of the ARPA Network", Digest of Papers, COMPCON73, San Francisco, February 1973.

<Kittner>. J.M. Kittner, J.S. Voorhees, "Regulatory and Policy Problems Presented by the Interdependence of Computer and Communications Services and Facilities", presented before the Federal Communications Commission, Docket No. 16979, Byron S. Adams Printing, Inc., Washington, D.C., March 1968.

<Kleinrock>. L. Kleinrock, "Analytic and Simulation Methods in Computer Networks Design", AFIPS Conference Proceedings, May 1970.

<Kleinrock1>. L. Kleinrock, "Communication Nets: Stochastic Message Flow and Delays", McGraw-Hill, 1964.

<Kleinrock2>. L. Kleinrock, S.S. Lam, "Approximations in the Infinite Population Model of the ARPANET Satellite System", ASS Note #17,NIC #11862, October 1972.

<Kleinrock3>. L. Kleinrock, S.S. Lam, "Packet-switching in a Slotted Satellite Channel", AFIPS Conference Proceedings, Volume 42, Page 703, June 1973.

<Kuo>. F.F. Kuo, N. Abramson, "Some Advances in Radio Communications for Computers", NIC #13643, Digest of Papers, COMPCON73, San Francisco, February 1973.

<Lampson>. B.W. Lampson, "Dynamic Protection Structures", AFIPS Conference Proceedings, November 1969.

<Lampson1>. B.W. Lampson, "Protection", Proceedings of the Fifth Princeton Conference on Information Sciences and Systems, Princeton University, 1971.

<Lee>. A.M. Lee, "Applied Queueing Theory", MacMillan, 1966.

Bibliography

<Liao>. H.H.J. Liao, "Multiple Access Channels", PhD Thesis, Technical Report A72-2, The ALOHA System, University of Hawaii, September 1972.

<Licklider>. J.C.R. Licklider, et al., "Techniques, Facilities, and Protocols for Dialogue and Interactive Cooperation through the ARPA Network", Internal Memorandum of the ARPA Network Working Group Workshop at MIT, October 1971.

<Lin>. S. Lin, "An Introduction to Error-Correction Codes", Prentice-Hall, 1970.

<Lu>. S. Lu, "Dynamic Analysis of Slotted ALOHA with Blocking", University of Hawaii, ASS Note #36, NIC #14790, March 1973.

<MAC>. "Proposal for Continuation of Research", MIT Project MAC, January 1972.

<Madnick>. S.E. Madnick, "Multi-Processor Software Lockout", Cambridge Scientific Center, IBM Technical Report #320-2027, April 1968.

<Manning>. "A Trans-Canada Computer Communications Network", Science Council of Canada, Report Number 13, Committee on Computer Applications and Technology, Project Officer Dr. Eric G. Manning, August 1971.

<Marill>. T. Marill, L.G. Roberts, "Toward a Cooperative Network of Time-Shared Computers", AFIPS Conference Proceedings, Volume 29, Page 425, November 1966.

<Mason>. W.E. Mason, et al., "Urban Cable Systems", The MITRE Corporation, M72-57, May 1972.

<McKenzie>. A.A. McKenzie, B.P. Cosell, J.M. McQuillan, M.J. Thrope, "The Network Control Center for the ARPA Network", International Conference on Computers and Communication, October 1972.

<McKenzie1>. A.A. McKenzie, "HOST/HOST Protocol for the ARPA Network", NIC #8246, January 1972.

Bibliography

<McKenzie2>. A. McKenzie, "HOST/HOST Protocol Design Considerations", International Network Working Group Note #16, NIC #13879, January 1973.

<McQuillan>. J.M. McQuillan, et al., "Improvements in the Design and Performance of the ARPA Network", AFIPS Conference Proceedings, December 1972.

<Metcalfe>. R.M. Metcalfe, "Some Historic Moments in Networking", RFC #89, NIC #5697, January 1971.

<Metcalfe1>. R.M. Metcalfe, "Using NETWRK: A Program Providing Terminal Access to the ARPA Computer Network", MIT Project MAC Dynamic Modeling/Computer Graphics System Document SYS.10.01, October 1971.

<Metcalfe2>. R.M. Metcalfe, G.J. Popek, "Concurrence Sensitive Task Models: A Research Report", Internal Technical Report at Harvard University, January 1970.

<Metcalfe3>. R.M. Metcalfe, "Strategies for Interprocess Communication in a Distributed Computing System", Proceedings of the Symposium on Computer-Communications Networks and Teletraffic, Polytechnic Press, New York, 1972.

<Metcalfe4>. R.M. Metcalfe, "Strategies for Operating Systems in Computer Networks", Proceedings of the National Conference of the ACM, Boston, August 1972.

<Metcalfe5>. B. Metcalfe, "System Programmer's Workshop Announcement", RFC #222, NIC #7621, September 1971, along with NWG Meeting announcements RFC #212, NIC #7192, and RFC #207, NIC #7178.

<Metcalfe6>. B. Metcalfe, "A TTL I/O Bus for the PDP-10", MIT Project MAC Dynamic Modeling/Computer Graphics System Document, July 1972.

<Metcalfe7>. B. Metcalfe, "An IMP Interface for the PDP-10", MIT Project MAC Dynamic Modeling/Computer Graphics System Document, July 1972.

<Metcalfe8>. B. Metcalfe, Editor, "Scenarios for Using the ARPANET at the International Conference on Computer Communication", NIC #11863, October 1972.

<Metcalfe9>. R.M. Metcalfe, "Steady-State Analysis of a Slotted and Controlled ALOHA System with Blocking", ARPANET Satellite System Note #16, NIC #11624, shortened for the Proceedings of the Sixth Hawaii International Conference on System Sciences, January 1973.

<Michener>. J.C. Michener, et al., "Graphics Protocol -- Level 0 Only", RFC #292, NIC #8302, January 1972.

<Mimno>. N.W. Mimno, et al., "Terminal Access to the ARPA Network: Experience and Improvements", Digest of Papers, COMPCON73, San Francisco, February 1973.

<Minsky>. M. Minsky, "Form and Content in Computer Science", 1970 ACM Turing Lecture, JACM, Volume 17, Number 2, April 1970.

<Mitchell>. L.B. Mitchell, "Cyclic Error-Control Codes", Automatic Electric Technical Journal, January 1967.

<NAC>. "Packet Radio -- Systems Considerations", Network Analysis Corporation, PR #5, NIC #13630, January 1973.

<NAC1>. "Comparison of Hop-by-Hop and End-to-End Acknowledgement Schemes", Network Analysis Corporation, PR #7, NIC #13632, January 1973.

<Newell>. A. Newell, et al., "Speech-Understanding Systems: Final Report of a Study Group", Carnegie-Mellon University, Computer Science Department, May 1971.

<Newkirk>. J. Newkirk, et al., "A Prototypical Implementation of the NCP", RFC #55, June 1970.

<Ornstein>. S.M. Ornstein, "The Terminal IMP for the ARPA Computer Network", AFIPS Conference Proceedings, May 1972.

<O'Sullivan>. T.C. O'Sullivan, R.M. Metcalfe, et al., "TELNET Protocol", RFC #158, NIC #6768, May 1971.

<O'Sullivan1>. T.C. O'Sullivan, R.M. Metcalfe, et al., "Discussion of TELNET Protocol", RFC #139, NIC #6717, May 1971.

<Pack>. C.D. Pack, "The Effects of Multiplexing on a Computer-Communications System", CACM, Volume 16, Number 3, March 1973.

<Padlipsky>. M.A. Padlipsky, "Early Project MAC ARPA Network Experiments", Project MAC Computer Networks Group, Memorandum Number 14, February 1971.

<Papert>. S. Papert, "The Computer as a Super-Toy", presented at the National Conference of the ACM, Boston, August 1972.

<Parkhill>. D.F. Parkhill, "The Challenge of the Computer Utility", Addison-Wesley Publishing Company, 1966.

<PCI>. Section 214 application to the Federal Communications Commission, Packet Communications, Inc., January 1973.

<Peterson>. W.W. Peterson, "Error-Correcting Codes", MIT Press, 1961.

<Postel>. J.B. Postel, "TELNET Protocol", RFC #318, NIC #9348, 1972.

<Postel1>. J.B. Postel, "Official Initial Connection Protocol", NIC #7101, NWG Document #2, June 1971.

<Postel2>. J.B. Postel, UCLA PhD Thesis in preparation.

<Poupon>. J. Poupon, "Experimental Control Structure of PPL", Report of the Center for Research in Computing Technology, Harvard University, 1971.

<Prenner>. C.J. Prenner, "Multi-Path Control Structures for Programming Languages", Report of the Center for Research in Computing Technology, Harvard University, 1972.

<Roberts>. L.G. Roberts, B.D. Wessler, "Computer Network Development to Achieve Resource Sharing", AFIPS Conference Proceedings, May 1970.

<Roberts1>. L.G. Roberts, "ARPA Network Implications", EDUCOM, Volume 6, Number 3, Pages 4-8, NIC #12982, Fall 1972.

<Roberts2>. L.G. Roberts, "Extensions of Packet Communication Technology to a Hand Held Personal Terminal", AFIPS Conference Proceedings, Volume 40, Page 295, May 1972.

<Roberts3>. L.G. Roberts, "Capture Effects on ALOHA Channels", presented at the Sixth Hawaii International Conference on System Sciences, January 1973, also ASS Note #8.

<Roberts4>. L.G. Roberts, "Interleaved Satellite Reservation System", ASS Note #31, December 1972, revised for NCC73, "Dynamic Allocation of Satellite Capacity through Packet Reservation", AFIPS Conference Proceedings, Volume 42, Page 711, June 1973.

<Rustin>. R. Rustin, Editor "Computer Networks", Courant Computer Science Symposium 3, Courant Institute of Mathematical Sciences, New York University, Prentice-Hall Series in Automatic Computation, December 1970.

<Rutledge>. R.M. Rutledge, et al., "An Interactive Network of Time-Sharing Computers", Proceedings of the 24th National Conference of the ACM, Page 431, 1969.

<Saaty>. T.L. Saaty, "Elements of Queueing Theory", McGraw-Hill, 1961.

<Saltzer>. J. H. Saltzer, "Traffic Control in a Multiplexed Computer System", MIT PhD Thesis, Project MAC Technical Report #30, July 1966.

<Samuel>. A.L. Samuel, "Time-Sharing on a Multiconsole Computer", MIT Project MAC Technical Report #17, March 1965.

<Schaffner>. S. C. Schaffner, C.R. Jones, K. Sattley, "AOSS -- Advanced Operations Support System for Small Computers", Applied Data Research, CA-7104-2211, April 1971.

<Schroeder>. M.D. Schroeder, J.H. Saltzer, "A Hardware Architecture for Implementing Protection Rings", Communications of the ACM, March 1972.

<Seidler>. J. Seidler, "Systemy Przesylania Informacji Cyfrowych", Wydawnictwa Naukowo-Techniczne, Warszawa, 1972.

<Seriff>. M.S. Seriff, "ARPANET HOST Availability Data", RFC #308, NIC #9259, March 1972.

<Smith>. T.L. Smith, "Transmission Parameters and Error Recovery Procedures for Inter-Computer Communications", MIT MS EE Thesis, January 1969.

<Smith1>. W.L. Smith, W.E. Wilkinson, "Congestion Theory", University of North Carolina Press, 1964.

<Sussman>. S.M. Sussman, "Analysis of the Pareto Model for Error Statistics on Telephone Circuits", IEEE Transactions on Communications Systems, March 1963.

<Taft>. E.A. Taft, T.A. Standish, "PPL User's Manual", Report of the Center for Research in Computing Technology, Harvard University, NIC #8255, January 1972.

<Thomas>. R. Thomas, "A Model for Process Representation and Synthesis", MIT PhD Thesis, Project MAC Technical Report #87, June 1971.

<Thomas1>. R.H. Thomas, D.A. Henderson, "MCROSS -- A Multi-Computer Programming System", AFIPS Conference Proceedings, Volume 40, Page 281, May 1972.

<Walden>. D.C. Walden, "A System for Interprocess Communication in a Resource Sharing Computer Network", RFC #62, NIC #4962, revised for CACM, Volume 15, Number 4, April 1972.

<Wang>. P.S. Wang, "Application of MACSYMA to an Asymptotic Expansion Problem", Proceedings of the National Conference of the ACM, Page 844, Boston, August 1972.

<Wegbreit>. B. Wegbreit, et al., "ECL Programmer's Manual", Report of the Center for Research in Computing Technology, Harvard University, September 1972.

<White>. J.E. White, "Network Specifications for Remote Job Entry and Remote Job Output Retrieval at UCSB", RFC #105, NIC #5775, March 1971.

<White1>. J.E. White, "Network Specifications for UCSB's Simple-Minded File System", RFC#122, NIC #5834, April 1971.

<Vyssotsky>. V.A. Vyssotsky, F.J. Corbato, R.M. Graham, "Structure of the Multics Supervisor", AFIPS Conference Proceedings, Volume 27-1, November 1965.

<Zeigler>. J.F. Zeigler, "Nodal Blocking in Large Networks", UCLA Computer Science Report Number UCLA-ENG 7167, October 1971.

Network Working Group
Request for Comments #62
August 3, 1970
The attached note supersedes NWG/RFC #61.

Dave Walden
Bolt Beranek and Newman

A System for Interprocess Communication in a Resource Sharing Computer Network

by

D. C. Walden

Bolt Beranek and Newman Inc. Cambridge, Massachusetts

1. Introduction

If you are working to develop methods of communications within a computer network, you can engage in one of two activities. You can work with others, actually constructing a computer network, being influenced, perhaps influencing your colleagues. Or you can construct an intellectual position of how things should be done in an ideal network, one better than the one you are helping to construct, and then present this position for the designers of future networks to study. The author has spent the past two years engaged in the first activity. This paper results from recent engagement in the second activity.

"A resource sharing computer network is defined to be a set of autonomous, independent computer systems, interconnected so as to permit each computer system to utilize all of the resources of the other computer systems much as it would normally call a subroutine." This definition of a network and the desirability of such a network is expounded upon by Roberts and Wessler in [9].

The actual act of resource sharing can be performed in two ways: in an *ad hoc* manner between all pairs of computer systems in the network; or according to a systematic network-wide standard. This paper develops one possible network-wide system for resource sharing.

I believe it is natural to think of resources as being associated with processes[1] and available only through communication with these processes. Therefore, I view the fundamental problem of resource sharing to be the problem of interprocess communication. I also share with Carr, Crocker, and Cerf [2] the view that interprocess communication over a network is a subcase of general interprocess communication in a multi-programmed environment.

These views have led me to perform a two-part study. First, a set of operations enabling interprocess communication within a single time-sharing system is constructed. This set of operations eschews many of the interprocess communication techniques currently in use within time-sharing systems — such as communication through shared memory — and relies instead on techniques that can be easily generalized to permit communication between remote processes. The second part of the study presents such a generalization. The application of this generalized system to the ARPA Computer Network [9] is also discussed.

The ideas enlarged upon in this paper came from many sources. Particularly influential were — 1) an early sketch of a Host protocol for the ARPA Network by S. Crocker of UCLA and W. Crowther of Bolt Beranek and Newman Inc. (BBN); 2) Ackerman and Plummer's paper on the MIT PDP-1 time-sharing system [1]; and 3) discussions with W. Crowther and R. Kahn of BBN about Host protocol, flow control, and message routing for the ARPA Network. Hopefully, there are also some original ideas in this note. I alone am responsible for the collection of all of these ideas into the system described herein, and I am therefore responsible for any inconsistencies or bugs in the system.

It must be emphasized that this paper does not represent an official BBN position on Host protocol for the ARPA Computer Network.

---

[1] Almost any of the common definitions of a process would suit true needs of this paper.

2. A System for Interprocess Communication within a Time-Sharing System

This section describes a set of operations enabling inter-process communication within a time-sharing system. Following the notation of [10], I call this interprocess communication facility an IPC. As an aid to the presentation of this IPC, a model for a time-sharing system is described; this model is then used to illustrate the use of the interprocess communication operations.

The model time-sharing system has two pieces: the monitor and the processes. The monitor performs such functions as switching control from one process to another process when a process has used "enough" time, fielding hardware interrupts, managing core and the swapping medium, controlling the passing of control from one process to another (i.e., protection mechanisms), creating processes, caring for sleeping processes, and providing to the processes a set of machine extending operations (often called Supervisor or Monitor Calls). The processes perform the normal user functions (user processes) as well as the functions usually thought of as being supervisor functions in a time-sharing system (system processes) but not performed by the monitor in the current model. A typical system process is the disc handler or the file system. System processes are probably allowed to execute in supervisor mode, and they actually execute I/O instructions and perform other privileged operations that user processes are not allowed to perform. In all other ways, user and system processes are identical. For reasons of efficiency, it may be useful to think of system processes as being locked in core.

Although they will be of concern later in this study, protection considerations are not my concern here: instead I will assume that all of the processes are "good" processes which never make any mistakes. If the reader needs a protection structure to keep in mind while he reads this note, the *capability* system developed in [1][3][7][8] should be satisfying.

Of the operations a process can call on the monitor to perform, six are of particular interest for providing a capability for interprocess communication.

RECEIVE. This operation allows a specified process to send a message to the process executing the RECEIVE. The operation has four parameters: the port (defined below) awaiting the message — the RECEIVE port; the port a message will be accepted from — the SEND port; a specification of the buffer available to receive the message; and a location to transfer to when the transmission is complete — the restart location.

SEND. This operation sends a message from the process executing the SEND to a specified process. It has four parameters: a port to send the message to — the RECEIVE port; the port the message is being sent from — the SEND port; a specification of the buffer containing the message to be sent; and the restart location.

RECEIVE ANY. This operation allows any process to send a message to the process executing the RECEIVE ANY. The operation has four parameters: the port awaiting the message — the RECEIVE port; a specification of the buffer available to receive the message; a restart location; and a location where the port which sent the message may be noted.

SEND FROM ANY. This operation allows a process to send a message to a process able to receive a message from any process. It has the same four parameters as SEND. (The necessity for this operation will be explained much later.)

SLEEP. This operation allows the currently running process to put itself to sleep pending the completion of an event. The operation has one optional parameter, an event to be waited for. An example event is the archival of a hardware interrupt. The monitor never unilaterally puts a process to sleep as a result of the process executing one of the above four operations; however, if a process is asleep when one of the above four operations is satisfied, the process is awakened.

UNIQUE. This operation obtains a unique number from the monitor.

A *port* is a particular data path to a process (a RECEIVE port) or from a process (a SEND port), and all ports have an associated unique *port number* which is used to identify the port. Ports are used in transmitting messages from one process to another in the following manner. Consider two processes, A and B, that wish to communicate. Process A executes a RECEIVE to port N from port M. Process B executes a SEND to port N from port M. The monitor matches up the port numbers and transfers the message from process B to process A. As soon as the buffer has been fully transmitted out of process B, process B is restarted at the location specified in the SEND operation. As soon as the message is fully received at process A, process A is restarted at the location specified in the RECEIVE operation. Just how the processes come by the correct port numbers with which to communicate with other processes is not the concern of the monitor — this problem is left to the processes.

Walden

When a SEND is executed, nothing happens until a matching RECEIVE is executed. Somewhere in the monitor there must be a table of port numbers associated with processes and restart locations. *The table entries are cleared after each SEND/ RECEIVE match is made.* If a proper RECEIVE is not executed for some time, the SEND is timed out after a while and the SENDing process is notified. If a RECEIVE is executed but the matching SEND does not happen for a long time, the RECEIVE is timed out and the RECEIVing process is notified.

The mechanism of timing out "unused" table entries is of little fundamental importance, merely providing a convenient method of garbage collecting the table. There is no problem if an entry is timed out prematurely, because the process can always re-execute the operation. However, the timeout interval should be long enough so that continual re-execution of an operation will cause little overhead.

A RECEIVE ANY never times out, but may be taken back using a supervisor call. A message resultant from a SEND FROM ANY is always sent immediately and will be discarded if a proper receiver does not exist. An error message is not returned and acknowledgment, if any, is up to the processes. If the table where the SEND and RECEIVE are matched up ever overflows, a process originating a further SEND or RECEIVE is notified just as if the SEND or RECEIVE timed out.

The *restart location* is an interrupt entrance associated with a pseudo interrupt local to the process executing the operation specifying the restart location. If the process is running when the event causing the pseudo interrupt occurs (for example, a message arrives satisfying a pending RECEIVE), the effect is exactly as if the hardware interrupted the process and transferred control to the restart location. Enough information is saved for the process to continue execution at the point it was interrupted after the interrupt is serviced. If the process is asleep, it is readied and the pseudo interrupt is saved until the process runs again and the interrupt is then allowed. Any RECEIVE or RECEIVE ANY message port may thus be used to provide process interrupts, event channels, process synchronation, message transfers, etc. The user programs what he wants.

It is left as an exercise to the reader to convince himself that the monitor he is saddled with can be made to provide the six operations described above — most monitors can since these are only additional supervisor calls.

An example. Suppose that our model time-sharing system is initialized to

159

have several processes always running. Additionally, these permanent processes have some universally known and permanently assigned ports.[2] Suppose that two of the permanently running processes are the logger-process and the teletype-scanner-process. When the teletype-scanner-process first starts running, it puts itself to sleep awaiting an interrupt from the hardware teletype scanner. The logger-process initially puts itself to sleep awaiting a message from the teletype-scanner-process via well-known permanent SEND and RECEIVE ports. The teletype-scanner-process keeps a table indexed by teletype number, containing in each entry a pair of port numbers to use to send characters from that teletype to a process and a pair of port numbers to use to receive characters for that teletype from a process. If a character arrives (waking up the teletype-scanner-process) and the process does not have any entry for that teletype, it gets a pair of unique numbers from the monitor (via UNIQUE) and sends a message containing this pair of numbers to the logger-process using the ports for which the logger-process is known to have a RECEIVE pending. The scanner-process also enters the pair of numbers in the teletype table, and sends the character and all future characters from this teletype to the port with the first number from the port with the second number. The scanner-process must also pass a second pair of unique numbers to the logger-process for it to use for teletype output and do a RECEIVE using these port numbers. When the logger-process receives the message from the scanner-process, it starts up a copy or what SDS 940 TSS [6] users call the executive[3], and passes the port numbers to this copy of the executive, so that this executive-process can also do its inputs and outputs to the teletype using these ports. If the logger-process wants to get a job number and password from the user, it can temporarily use the port numbers to conmunicate with the user before it passes them on to the executive. The scanner-process could always use the same port numbers for a particular teletype; as long as the numbers were passed on to only one copy of the executive at a time.

It is important to distinguish between the act of passing a port from one process to another and the act of passing a port number from one process to another. In the previous example, where characters from a particular teletype

---

[2] Or perhaps there is only one permanently known port, which belongs to a directory-process that keeps a table of permanent-process/well-known-port associations.

[3] That program which prints file directories, tells who is on other teletypes, runs subsystems, etc.

are sent either to the logger-process or an executive-process by the teletype-scanner-process, the SEND port always remains in the teletype-scanner-process while the RECEIVE port moves from the logger-process to the executive-process. On the other hand, the SEND port number is passed between the logger-process and the executive-process to enable the RECEIVE process to do a RECEIVE from the correct SEND port. It is crucial that, once a process transfers a port to some other process, the first process no longer use the port. We could add a mechanism that enforces this. The protected object system of [9] is one such mechanism. Using this mechanism, a process executing a SEND would need a capability for the SEND port and only one capability for this SEND port would exist in the system at any given time. A process executing a RECEIVE would be required to have a capability for the RECEIVE port, and only one capability for this RECEIVE port would exist at a given time. Without such a protection mechanism, a port implicitly moves from one process to another by the processes merely using the port at disjoint times even if the port's number is never explicitly passed.

Of course, if the protected object system is available to us, there is really no need for two port numbers to be specified before a transmission can take place. The fact that a process knows an existing RECEIVE port number could be considered *prima facie* evidence of the process' right to send to that port. The difference between RECEIVE and RECEIVE ANY ports then depends solely on the number of copies of a particular port number that have been passed out. A system based on this approach should clearly be preferable to the one described here if it was possible to assume that all autonomous time-sharing systems in a network would adopt this protection mechanism. If this assumption cannot be made, it seems more practical to require both port numbers.

Note that in the interprocess communication system (IPC) being described here, when two processes wish to communicate they set up the connection themselves, and they are free to do it in a mutually convenient manner. For instance, they can exchange port numbers or one process can pick all the port numbers and instruct the other process which to use. However, in a particular implementation of a time-sharing system, the builders of the system might choose to restrict the processes' execution of SENDs and RECEIVEs and might forbid arbitrary passing around of ports and port numbers, requiring instead that the monitor be called (or some other special program) to perform these functions.

Flow control is provided in this IPC by the simple method of never starting data transmission resultant from a SEND from one process until a RECEIVE is executed by the receiver. Of course, interprocess messages may also be sent back and forth suggesting that a process stop sending or that space be allocated.

Generally, well-known permanently-assigned ports are used via RECEIVE ANY and SEND FROM ANY. The permanent ports will most often be used for starting processes and, consequently, little data will be sent via them. If a process is running (perhaps asleep), and has a RECEIVE ANY pending, then any process knowing the receive port number can talk to that process without going through loggers. This is obviously essential within a local time-sharing system and seems very useful in a more general network if the ideal of resource sharing is to be reached. For instance, in a resource sharing network, the programs in the subroutine libraries at all sites might have RECEIVE ANYs always pending over permanently assigned ports with well-known port numbers. Thus, to use a particular network resource such as a matrix inversion subroutine at a site with special matrix manipulation hardware, a process running anywhere in the network can send a message to the matrix inversion subroutine containing the matrix to be inverted and the port numbers to be used for returning the results.

An additional example demonstrates the use of the FORTRAN compiler. We have already explained how a user sits down at his teletype and gets connected to an executive. We go on from there. The user is typing in and out of the executive which is doing SENDs and RECEIVEs. Eventually the user types RUN FORTRAN, and the executive asks the monitor to start up a copy of the FORTRAN compiler and passes to FORTRAN as start up parameters the port numbers the executive was using to talk to the teletype. (Thus, at least conceptually, FORTRAN is passed a port at which to RECEIVE characters from the teletype and a port from which to SEND characters to the teletype.) FORTRAN is, of course, expecting these parameters and does SENDs and RECEIVEs via the indicated ports to discover from the user what input and output files the user wants to use. FORTRAN types INPUT FILE? to the user, who responds; F001. FORTRAN then sends a message to the file-system-process, which is asleep waiting for something to do. The message is sent via well-known ports and it asks the file system to open F001 for input. The message also contains a pair of port numbers that the file-system process can use to send its reply. The file-system looks up F001, opens it for input, make some entries in its open file tables, and sends back to FORTRAN a message containing the port numbers that FORTRAN can use to read the file. The same procedure is followed for the output file. When the compilation is complete, FORTRAN returns the teletype port numbers (and the ports) back to the executive that has been asleep waiting for a message from FORTRAN, and then FORTRAN halts itself. The file-system-process goes back to sleep when it has nothing else to do[4].

Again, the file-system process can keep a small collection of port numbers which it uses over and over if it can get file system users to return the port numbers when they have finished with them. Of course, when this collection of port numbers has eventually dribbled away, the file system can get some new unique numbers from the monitor.

3. A System for Interprocess Communication Between Remote Processes

The IPC described in the previous section easily generalizes to allow interprocess communication between processes at geographically different locations as, for example, within a computer network.

Consider first a simple configuration of processes distributed around the points of a star. At each point of the star there is an autonomous operating system[5]. A rather large, smart computer system, called the Network Controller, exists at the center of the star. No processes can run in this center system, but rather it should be thought of as an extension of the monitor of each of the operating systems in the network.

If the Network Controller is able to perform the operations SEND, RECEIVE, SEND FROM ANY, RECEIVE ANY, and UNIQUE and if all of the monitors in all of the time-sharing systems in the network do not perform these operations themselves but rather ask the Network Controller to perform these

---

[4] The reader should have noticed by now that I do not like to think of a new process (consisting of a near conceptual copy of a program) being started up each time another user wishes to use the program. Rather, I like to think of the program as a single process which knows it is being used simultaneously by many other processes and consciously multiplexes among the users or delays service to users until it can get around to them.

[5] I use operating system rather than time-sharing system in this section to point up the fact that the autonomous systems at the network nodes may be either full blown time-sharing systems in their own right, an individual process in a larger geographically distributed time-sharing system, or merely autonomous sites wishing to communicate.

operations for them, then the problem of interprocess communication between remote processes is solved. No further changes are necessary since the Network Controller can keep track of which RECEIVEs have been executed and which SENDs have been executed and match them up just as the monitor did in the model time-sharing system. A network-wide port numbering scheme is also possible with the Network Controller knowing where (i.e., at which site) a particular port is at a particular time.

Next, consider a more complex network in which there is no common center point, making it necessary to distribute the functions performed by the Network Controller among the network nodes. In the rest of this section I will show that it is possible to efficiently and conveniently distribute the functions performed by the star Network Controller among the many network sites and still enable general interprocess communication between remote processes.

Some changes must be made to each of the four SEND/RECEIVE operations described above to adapt them for use in a distributed Network Controller. To RECEIVE is added a parameter specifying a site to which the RECEIVE is to be sent. To the SEND FROM ANY and SEND messages is added a site to send the SEND to although this is normally the local site. Both RECEIVE and RECEIVE ANY have added the provision for obtaining the source site of any received message. Thus, when a RECEIVE is executed, the RECEIVE is sent to the site specified, possibly a remote site. Concurrently a SEND is sent to the same site, normally the local site of the process executing the SEND. At this site, called the rendezvous site, the RECEIVE is matched with the proper SEND and the message transmission is allowed to take place from the SEND site to the site from whence the RECEIVE came.

A RECEIVE ANY never leaves its originating site and therein lies the necessity for SEND FROM ANY, since it must be possible to send a message to a RECEIVE ANY port and not have the message blocked waiting for a RECEIVE at the sending site. It is possible to construct a system so the SEND/RECEIVE rendezvous takes place at the RECEIVE site and eliminate the SEND FROM ANY operation, but in my judgment the ability to block a normal SEND transmission at the source site more than makes up for the added complexity.

At each site a rendezvous table is kept. This table contains an entry for each unmatched SEND or RECEIVE received at that site and also an entry for all RECEIVE ANYs given at that site. A matching SEND/RECEIVE pair is cleared from the table as soon as the match takes place. As in the similar table kept in the model time-sharing system, SEND and RECEIVE entries are timed out if unmatched for too long and the originator is notified. RECEIVE ANY entries are cleared from the table when a fulfilling message arrives.

The final change necessary to distribute the Network Controller functions is to give each site a portion of the unique numbers to distribute via its UNIQUE operation. I'll discuss this topic further below.

To make it clear to the reader how the distributed Network Controller works, an example follows. The details of what process picks port numbers, etc., are only exemplary and are not a standard specified as part of the IPC.

Suppose that, for two sites in the network, K and L, process A at site K wishes to communicate with process B at site L. Process B has a RECEIVE ANY pending at port M.

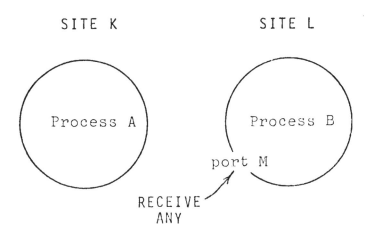

Process A, fortunately, knows of the existence of port M at site L and sends a message using the SEND FROM ANY operation from port N to port M. The message contains two port numbers ard instructions for process B to SEND messages for process A to port P from port Q. Site K's site number is appended to this message along with the message's SEND port N.

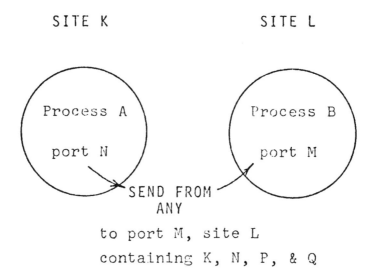

Process A now executes a RECEIVE at port P from port Q. Process A specifies the rendezvous site to be site L.

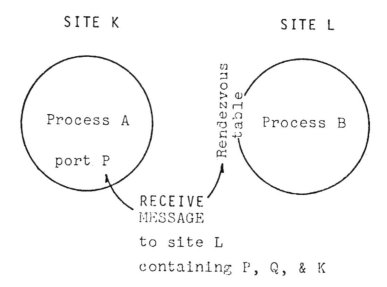

A RECEIVE message is sent from site X to site L and is entered in the rendezvous table at site L. At some other time, process B executes a SEND to port P from port Q specifying site L as the rendezvous site.

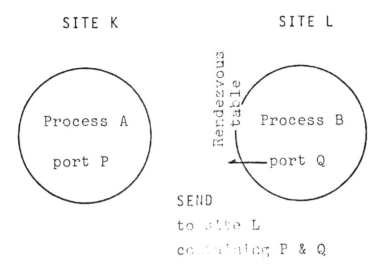

A rendezvous is made, the rendezvous table entry is cleared, and the transmission to port P at site K takes place. The SEND site number (and conceivably the SEND port number) is appended to the messages of the transmission for the edification of the receiving process.

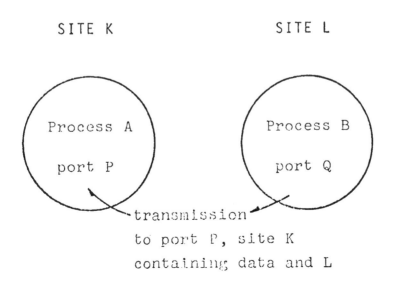

Process B may simultaneously wish to execute a RECEIVE from port N at port M.

Note that there is only one important control message in this system which moves between sites, the type of message that is called a Host/Host protocol message in [2]. This control message is the RECEIVE message. There are two other possible intersite control messages: an error message to the originating site when a RECEIVE or SEND is timed out, and the SEND message in the rare case when the rendezvous site is not the SEND site. There must also be a standard format for messages between ports. For example, the following:

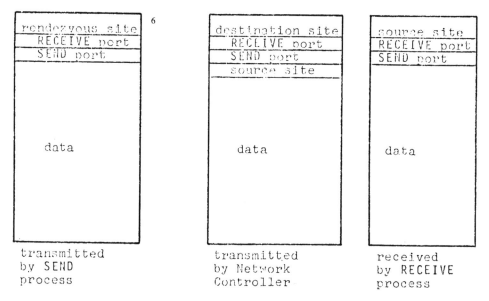

rendezvous site	6
RECEIVE port	
SEND port	
data	

transmitted
by SEND
process

| destination site |
| RECEIVE port |
| SEND port |
| source site |
| data |

transmitted
by Network
Controller

| source site |
| RECEIVE port |
| SEND port |
| data |

received
by RECEIVE
process

In the model time-sharing system it was possible to pass a port from process to process. This is still possible with a distributed Network Controller.

Remember that, for a message to be sent from one process to another, a SEND to port M from port N and a RECEIVE at port M from port N must rendezvous, normally at the SEND site. Both processes keep track of where they think the rendezvous site is and supply this site as a parameter of appropriate operations. The RECEIVE process thinks it is the SEND site and the SEND process normally thinks it is the SEND site also. Since once a SEND and a

---

6 For a SEND FROM ANY message, the rendezvous site is the destination site.

RECEIVE rendezvous the transmission is sent to the source of the RECEIVE and the entry in the rendezvous table is cleared and must be set up again for each further transmission from N to M, it is easy for a RECEIVE port to be moved. If a process sends both the port numbers and the rendezvous site number to a new process at some other site which executes a RECEIVE using these same old port numbers and rendezvous site specification, the SENDer never knows the RECEIVEr has moved. It is slightly harder for a SEND port to move. However, if it does, the pair of port numbers that has been used for a SEND and the original rendezvous site number are passed to the new site. The process at the new SEND site specifies the old rendezvous site with the first SEND from the new site. The RECEIVE process will also still think the rendezvous site is the old site, so the SEND and RECEIVE will meet at the old site. When they meet, the entry in the table at that site is cleared, and both the SEND and RECEIVE messages are sent to the new SEND site just as if they had been destined for there in the first place. The SEND and RECEIVE then meet again at the new rendezvous site and transmission may continue as if the port had never moved. Since all transmissions contain the source site number, further RECEIVEs will be sent to the near rendezvous site. It is possible to discover that this special manipulation must take place because a SEND message is received at a site that did not originate the SEND message[7]. Note that the SEND port and the RECEIVE port can move concurrently.

Of course, all of this could have also been done if the processes had sent messages back and forth announcing any potential moves and the new site numbers.

A problem that may have occurred to the reader is how the SEND and RECEIVE buffers get matched for size. The easiest solution would be to require that all buffers have a common size, but this is unacceptable since it does not easily extend to a situation where processes in autonomous operating systems are attempting to communicate. A second solution is for the processes to pass messages specifying buffer sizes. If this solution is adopted, excessive data sent from the SEND process and unable to fit into the RECEIVE buffer is discarded

---

[7] For readers familiar with the once-proposed re-connection scheme for the ARPA Network, the above system is simple, comparatively, because there are no permanent connections to break and move; that is, connections only exist fleetingly in the system described here and can therefore be remade between any pair of processes which at any time happen to know each other's port numbers and have some clue where they each are.

and the RECEIVE process notified. The solution has great appeal on account of its simplicity. A third solution would be for the RECEIVE buffer size to be passed to the SEND site with RECEIVE message and to notify the SEND process when too much data is sent or even to pass the RECEIVE buffer size on to the SEND process. This last method would also permit the Network Controller at the SEND site to make two or more SENDs out of one, if that was necessary to match a smaller RECEIVE buffer size.

The maintenance of unique numbers is also a problem when the processes are geographically distributed. Three solutions to this problem are presented here. The first possibility is for the autonomous operating systems to ask the Network Controller for the unique number originally and then guarantee the integrity of any unique numbers currently owned by local processes and programs using whatever means are at the operating system's disposal. In this case, the Network Controller would provide a method for a unique number to be sent from one site to another and would vouch for the number's identity at the new site. The second method is simply to give the unique numbers to the processes that are using them, depending on the non-malicious behavior of the processes to preserve the unique numbers, or if an accident should happen, the *two* passwords (SEND and RECEIVE port numbers) that are required to initiate a transmission. If the unique numbers are given out in a non-sequential manner and are reasonably long (say 32 bits), there is little danger. In the final method, a user identification is included in the port numbers and the individual operating systems guarantee the integrity of these identification bits. Thus a process, while not able to be sure that the correct port is transmitting to him, can be sure that some port of the correct user is transmitting. This is the so-called virtual net concept suggested by W. Crowther [2][8].

A third difficult problem arises when remote processes wish to communicate, the problem of maintaining high bandwidth connections between the remote processes. The solution to this problem lies in allowing the processes considerable information about the state of an ongoing transmission. First,, we examine a SEND process in detail. When a process executes a SEND, the local portion of the Network Controller passes the SEND on to the rendezvous site, normally the local site. When a RECEIVE arrives matching a pending SEND,

---

[8] Crowther says this is not the virtual net concept.

the Network Controller notifies the SEND process by causing an interrupt to the specified restart location. Simultaneously the Network Controller starts shipping the SEND buffer to the RECEIVE site. When transmission is complete, a flag is set which the SEND process can test. While a transmission is taking place, the process may ask the Network Controller to perform other operations, including other SENDs. A second SEND over a pair of ports already in the act of transmission is noted and the SEND becomes active as soon as the first transmission is complete. A third identical SEND results in an error message to the SENDing process. Next, we examine a RECEIVE process in detail. When a process executes a RECEIVE, the RECEIVE is sent to the rendezvous site. When data resultant from this RECEIVE starts to arrive at the RECEIVE site, the RECEIVE process is notified via an interrupt to the specified restart location. When the transmission is complete, a flag is set which the RECEIVE process can test. A second RECEIVE over the same port pair is allowed. A third results in an error message to the RECEIVE process. Thus, there is sufficient machinery to allow a pair of processes always to have both a transmission in progress and the next one pending. Therefore, no efficiency is lost. On the other hand, each transmission must be preceded by a RECEIVE into a specified buffer, thus continuing to provide complete flow control.

4. A Potential Application

Only one resource sharing computer network currently exists, the ARPA Computer Network. In this section, I discuss application of the system described in this paper to the ARPA Network [2][5][9].

The ARPA Network currently incorporates ten sites spread across the United States. Each site consists of one to three (potentially four) independent computer systems called Hosts and one communications computer system called an IMP. All of the Hosts at a site are directly connected to the IMP. The IMPs themselves are connected together by 50-kilobit phone lines (much higher rate lines are a potential), although each IMP is connected to only one to five other IMPs. The IMPs provide a communications subnet through which the Hosts communicate. Data is sent through the communications subnet in messages of arbitrary size (currently about 8000 bits) called *network messages*. When a network message is received by the IMP at the destination site, that IMP sends an acknowledgment, called an *RFNM,* to the source site.

A system for interprocess communication for the ARPA Network (let us call this IPC for ARPA) is currently being designed by the Network Working Group, under the chairmanship of S. Crocker of UCLA. Their design is somewhat constrained by the communications subnet [5][9]. I would like to compare point-by-point IPC for ARPA with the one developed in this paper; however, such a comparison would first require description here, almost from scratch, of the current state of IPC for ARPA since very little up-to-date information about IPC for ARPA appears in the open literature [2]. Also, IPC for ARPA is quite complex and the working documents describing it now run to many hundred pages, making any description lengthy and inappropriate for this paper [10]. Therefore, I shall make only a few scattered comparisons of the two systems, the first of which are implicit in this paragraph.

The interprocess communication system being developed for the ARPA Network comes in several almost distinct pieces: The Host/IMP protocol, IMP/IMP protocol, and the Host/Host protocol. The IMPs have sole responsibility for correctly transmitting bits from one site to another. The Hosts have sole responsibility for making interprocess connections. Both the Host and IMP are concerned and take a little responsibility for flow control and message sequencing. Application of the interprocess communication system described in this paper leads me to make a different allocation of responsibility. The IMP still continues to move bits from one site to another correctly but the Network Controller also resides in the IMP, and flow control is completely in the hands of the processes running in the Hosts, although using the mechanisms provided by the IMPs.

The IMPs provide the SEND, RECEIVE, SEND FROM ANY, RECEIVE ANY, and UNIQUE operations in slightly altered forms for the Hosts and also maintain the rendezvous tables, including moving of SEND ports when necessary. Putting these operations in the IMP requires the Host/Host protocol program to be written only once, rather than many times as is currently being done in the ARPA Network. It is perhaps useful to step through the five operations again.

---

[9] As one of the builders of the ARPA communications subnet, I am partially responsible for these constraints.

[10] The reader having access to the ARPA working documents may want to read *Specifications for the Interconnection of a Host to an IMP*, BBN Report No. 1822; and ARPA Network Working Group Notes #36, 37, 38, 39, 42, 44, 46, 47, 48, 49, 50, 54, 55, 56, 57, 58, 59, 60.

SEND. The Host gives the IMP a SEND port number, a RECEIVE port number, the rendezvous site, and a buffer specification (e.g., start and end, or beginning and length). The SEND is sent to the rendezvous site IMP, normally the local IMP. When a matching RECEIVE arrives at the local IMP, the Host is notified of the RECEIVE port of the just arrived message. This port number is sufficient to identify the SENDing process, although a given operating system may have to keep internal tables mapping this port number into a useful internal process identifier. Simultaneously, the IMP begins to ask the Host for specific pieces of the SEND buffer, sending these pieces as network messages to the destination site. If an RFNM is not received for too long, implying a network message has been lost in the network, the Host is asked for the same data again and it is retransmitted[11]. Except for the last piece of a buffer, the IMP requests pieces from the Host which are common multiples of the word size of the source Host, IMP, and destination Host. This avoids mid-transmission word alignment problems.

RECEIVE. The Host gives the IMP a SEND port, a RECEIVE port, a rendezvous site, and a buffer description. The RECEIVE message is sent to the rendezvous site. As the network messages making up a transmission arrive for the RECEIVE port, they are passed to the Host along with RECEIVE port number (and perhaps the SEND port nunber), and an indication to the Host where to put this data in its input buffer. When the last network message of the SEND buffer is passed into the Host, it is marked accordingly and the Host can then detect this. (It is conceivable that the RECEIVE message could also allocate a piece of network bandwidth while making its network traverse to the rendezvous site.)

RECEIVE ANY. The Host gives the IMP a RECEIVE port and a buffer descriptor. This works the same as RECEIVE but assumes the local site to be the rendezvous site.

SEND FROM ANY. The Host gives the IMP RECEIVE and SEND ports, the destination site, and a buffer descriptor. The IMP requests and transmits the buffer as fast as possible. A SEND FROM ANY for a non-existent port is discarded at the destination site.

In the ARPA Network, the Hosts are required by the IMPs to physically

---

[11] This also allows messages to be completely thrown away by the IMP subnet if that should ever be useful.

break their transmissions into network messages, and successive messages of a single transmission must be delayed until the RFNM is received for the previous message. In the system described here, since RFNMs are tied to the transmission of a particular piece of buffer and since the Hosts allow the IMPs to reassemble buffers in the Hosts by the IMP telling the Host where to put each buffer piece, then pieces of a single buffer can be transmitted in parallel network messages and several RFNMs can be outstanding simultaneously. This enables The Hosts to deal with transmissions of more natural sizes and higher bandwidth for a single transmission.

For additional efficiency, the IMP might know the approximate time it takes for a RECEIVE to get to a particular other site and warn the Host to wake up a process shortly before the arrival of a message for that process is imminent.

5. Conclusion

Since the system described in this paper has not been implemented, I have no clearly demonstrable conclusions nor any performance reports. Instead, I conclude with four openly subjective claims:

1) The interprocess communication system described in Section 2 is simpler and more general than most existing systems of equivalent power and is more powerful than most intra-time-sharing system communication systems currently available.

2) Time-sharing systems structured like the model in Section 2 should be studied by designers of time-sharing systems who may see a computer network in their future, as structure seems to enable joining a computer network with a minimum of difficulty.

3) As computer networks become more common, remote interprocess communication systems like the one described in Section 3 should be studied. The system currently being developed for ARPA is a step in the wrong direction, being addressed, in my opinion, more to communication between monitors than to communication between processes and consequently subverting convenient resource sharing.

4) The application of the system as described in Section 4 is much simpler to implement and more powerful than the system currently being constructed for the ARPA Network, and I suggest that implementation of my method be seriously considered for adoption by the ARPA Network.

References

1. Ackerman, W., and Plummer, W. An implementation of a multi-processing computer system. Proc. ACM Symp. on Operating System Principles, Gatlinsburg, Tenn., Oct. 1–4, 1967.

2. Carr, C., Crocker, S., and Cerf, V. Host/Host communication protocol in the ARPA network. Proc. AFIPS 1970 Spring Joint Comput. Conf., Vol. 36, AFIPS Press, Montvale, N.J., pp. 589–597.

3. Dennis, J., and VanHorn, E. Programming semantics for multiprogrammed computations. *Comm ACM, 9,* 3 (March, 1965), 143–155.

4. Hansen, P.B. The nucleus of a multiprogramming system. *Comm. ACM 13,* 4 (April, 1970), 238–241, 250.

5. Heart, F., Kahn, R., Ornstein, S., Crowther, W., and Walden, D. The interface message processor for the ARPA computer network. Proc. AFIPS 1970 Spring Joint Comput. Conf., Vol. 36, AFIPS Press, Montvale, N.J., pp 551–567.

6. Lampson, B. *SDS 940 Lectures,* circulated informally.

7. ———. An overview of the CSL time-sharing system. Computer Center, University of California, Berkeley, Calif.

8. ———. Dynamic protection structures. Proc. AFIPS 1969 Fall Joint Comput. Conf., Vol. 35, AFIPS Press, Montvale, N. J., pp. 27–38.

9. Roberts, L., and Wessler, B. Computer network development to achieve resource sharing. Proc. AFIPS 1970 Spring Joint Comput. Conf., Vol. 36, AFIPS Press, Montvale, N.J., pp. 543–549.

10. Spier, M., and Organick, E. The MULTICS interprocess communication facility. Proc. ACM Second Symp. on Operating Systems Principles, Princeton University, Oct. 20–22, 1969.

Network Working Group
Request For Comments #89
NIC 5697

Bob Metcalfe
19 Jan. 1971

Some Historic Moments in Networking

While awaiting the completion of an interim network control program (INCP) for the MIT MAC Dynamic Modeling/Computer Graphics PDP-6/10 System (MITDG), we were able to achieve a number of 'historic moments in networking' worthy of some comment. First, we were able to connect an MITDG terminal to a Multics process making it a Multics terminal. Second, we successfully attached an MITDG terminal to the Harvard PDP-10 System thereby enabling automatic remote use of the Harvard System for MIT. Third, we developed primitive mechanisms through which remotely generated programs and data could be transmitted to our system, executed, and returned. Using these mechanisms in close cooperation with Harvard, we received graphics programs and 3D data from Harvard's PDP-1, processed them repeatedly using our Evans & Sutherland Line Drawing System (the E&S), and transmitted 2D scope data to Harvard's PDP-1 for display.

The IINCP

Our experiments were run on the MITDG PDP-6/10 using what we have affectionately called our 'interim interim NCP' (IINCP). Under the IINCP the IMP Interface is treated as a single-user I/O device which deals in raw network messages. The software supporting necessary system calls includes little more than the basic interrupt-handling and buffering schemes to be used later by the NCP. In short, the user-level programs which brought us to our historic moments were written close to the hardware with full knowledge of IMP-HOST Protocol (BBN 1822). When the INCP and NCP are completed, these programs can be pruned considerably (80%). The exercise of writing programs which conform to IMP-HOST Protocol was not at all wasted. Only now can those of us who are not writing the NCP begin to grasp the full meaning of RFNM's and their use in flow control. The penalties for ignoring an impatient IMP, for failing to send NOOPS (NO-OPS) when starting up, and for blasting data onto the Network without regard for RFNM's are now well understood.

The Multics Connection

Our quest for historic moments began with the need to demonstrate that the complex hardware-software system separating MITDG and Multics was operative and understood. A task force (Messrs. Bingham, Brodie, Knight, Metcalfe, Meyer, Padlipsky and Skinner) was commissioned to establish a 'polite conversation' between a Multics terminal and an MITDG terminal.

It was agreed that messages would be what we call 'network ASCII messages': 7-bit ASCII characters right-adjusted in 8-bit fields having the most significant bit set, marking, and padding. In that Multics is presently predisposed toward line-oriented half-duplex terminals, it was decided that all transmissions would end with the Multics EOL character (ASCII <LINE FEED>). To avoid duplicating much of the INCP in our experiment, the PDP-10 side of the connection was freed by convention from arbitrary bit-stream concatenation requirements and was permitted to associate logical message boundaries with network message boundaries (sic). The 'polite conversation' was thus established and successful.

Multics, then, connected the conversation to its command processor and the PDP-10 terminal suddenly became a Multics terminal. But, not quite:

First, in the resulting MITDG-Multics connection there was no provision for a remote QUIT, which in Multics is not an ASCII character. This is a problem for Multics. It would seem that an ASCII character or the network's own interrupt control message could be given QUIT significance.

Second, our initial driver program did not provide for RUBOUT. Because the Multics network input stream bypassed the typewriter device interface module (TTYDIM), line canonicalization was not performed. In a more elegant implementation, line canonicalization could be done at Multics, providing the type-in editing conventions familiar to Multics users. We fixed this problem hastily by having our driver program do local RUBOUT editing during line assembly, thus providing type-in editing conventions familiar to MITDG users. It is clearly possible to do both local type-in editing and distant-host type-in editing.

Third, we found that because of the manner in which our type-in entered the Multics system under the current network interface (i.e. not through TTYDIM), our remotely controlled processes were classified 'non-interactive' and thus fell to the bottom of Multics queues giving us slow response. This problem can be easily fixed.

The Harvard Connection

Connecting MITDG terminals to Multics proved to be easy in that the character-oriented MITDG system easily assembled lines for the Multics line-oriented system. We (Messrs. Barker, Metcalfe) decided, therefore, that it would be worthwhile to connect the MITDG system to another character-oriented system, namely Harvard's PDP-10. This move was also motivated by MITDG's desire to learn more about Harvard's new language systems via MITDG's own consoles.

It was found that Harvard had already provided an ASCII network interface to their system which accepted IMP-Teletype style messages as standard. We quickly rigged up an IMP-Teletype message handler at MITDG and were immediately compatible and connected. But not quite:

First, Harvard runs the Digital Equipment Corporation (DEC) time-sharing system on their PDP-10 which has <control-C> as a QUIT character and <control-Z> as an end-of-file (EOF). MITDG runs the MAC Incompatible Time-sharing System (ITS) which has <control-Z> as a QUIT character and <control-C> as an EOF. This control character mismatch is convenient in the sense that typing <control-C> while connected to the Harvard system through MITDG causes the right thing to happen—causes the execution of programs at Harvard to QUIT, as opposed to causing the driver program at MITDG to QUIT. If, however, a Harvard program were to require that an EOF be typed, typing <control-Z> would cause ITS to stop the driver program in its tracks, leaving the Harvard EOF wait unsatisfied and the MITDG-Harvard connection severed.

Second, the Harvard system has temporarily implemented this remote network console interface feature using a DEC style pseudo-teletype (PTY). This device vis-a-vis the DEC system behaves as a half-duplex terminal which wakes up on a set of 'break characters' (e.g., return, altmode) affording us an opportunity for an interesting experiment. The use of DDT (Dynamic Debugging Tool) is thereby restricted (though not prevented) in that break characters must be scattered throughout a DDT interaction to bring the PTY to life to cause DDT to do the right thing. For example, to examine the contents of a core location one needs to type 'addr/<altmode>' (address slash altmode) the altmode being only a call-to-action to the PTY. To alter the contents of the opened location, one must then type '<rub-out>contents<return>'; the <rub-out> character deletes the previous action <alt-mode>, the contents are stashed in the open address, and <return> signals the close of the address and PTY wake-up. It would seem that DDT is a program that will separate the men from the boys in networking.

Third, it was found that the response from the Harvard system at MITDG was seemingly as fast as could be expected from one of their own consoles. This fact is particularly exciting to those who don't have a feel for network transit times when it is pointed out that such response was generated through two time-sharing systems, three user level processes, and three IMPs, all connected in series.

The Harvard-MIT Graphics Experiment

At Harvard are a PDP-10 Time-sharing System and a graphics oriented PDP-1, both connected to Harvard's IMP. At MITDG are a PDP-6/10 Time-sharing System and an E&S Line Drawing System. It was felt (Messrs. Barker, Cohen, McQuillan, Metcalfe, and Taft) that the time had come to demonstrate that the network could make remote resources available -- to give Harvard access to the E&S at MITDG via the network. The protocol for such use of the network was as follows: (1) MITDG starts its network monitor program listening. (2) Harvard starts its PDP-10 transmitting a core image containing an arbitrary PDP-10 program (with an embedded E&S program in this case). (3) MITDG receives the core image from Harvard and places it in its memory at the starting address specified, collecting messages and concatenating them appropriately. (There was no word-length mismatch problem.) (4) Upon collecting a complete image (word count sent first along with starting address), MITDG stashes its own return address in a specified location of the transmitted program's image and transfers control to another image location. (5) Upon getting control at

180

MITDG, the transmitted program executes (in this case sets up and runs an E&S program) and before returning to the MITDG network monitor stashes in specified locations of its image the beginning and ending addresses of its results. (6) With control returned, the MITDG monitor program then transmits the results to a listening host which makes good use of them (in this case a PDP-1 which displays them). (7) Then the MITDG program either terminates, returns control back to the image (as in this case), or waits for more data and/or program. The protocol was implemented in the hosts and used to run a Harvard-assembled version of the E&S Aircraft Carrier Program (written originally by Harvard's Prof. Cohen) at MITDG and to display the resulting dynamic display on Harvard's PDP-1 driven DEC scopes. The Carrier Program was 'flown' from MITDG and the changing views thus generated appeared both at MITDG and Harvard. The picture was observed to change (being transmission limited) on the order of twice each second (perhaps less often). But all was not rosy:

First, it was observed that during the experiment, prompting messages to the IMP-Teletypes were often garbled. Most of the garbling can be attributed to the ASR-33 itself, some cannot. There were no errors detected during data transmissions not involving the IMP-Teletypes.

Second, during attempts to fly the Carrier from Harvard, we stumbled across a yet undiagnosed intermittent malfunction of (presumably) the MITDG hardware and/or software which caused our network connection to be totally shut down by the system during bi-directional transmission. This problem is currently under investigation.

Third, the response of the total system was slow compared to that required to do real-time dynamic graphics. One would expect that if this limitation is to be overcome, higher bandwidth transmission lines, faster host response to network messages, and/or perhaps a message priority system will be required.

General Comments

In producing 'network ASCII messages' we were required to bend over backwards to insert marking so that our last data bit could fall on a word boundary. Surely there must be a better way. The double padding scheme and its variants with or without marking should be considered. Given the current hardware, it would seem that double padding with marking would be an improvement. A simple (?) fix to host IMP interfaces enabling them to send only good

36-Bit Words Transmitted
From Harvard's PDP-10 to
MITG's PDP-10

-count	origin-1

Image control word.

Image:

start address of results

Image +1:

end address of results

Filled in by
Harvard's program
during its execution.

Image +2:

-------unused-------

Image +3:

program stop address

Image +4:

program start address

Filled in by MITDG
for return of control.

Image +5:

Image control word
and image arrive in
network size buffers
which are stripped of
marking and padding
and concatenated.

36-Bit Words Transmitted
From MITG's PDP-10 to
Harvard's PDP-1

	count

First word of results
specified in Image+0.

results

Last word of results
specified in Image+1

182

data from a partially filled last word would permit a further improvement: marking and host-supplied single padding.

In these initial experiments Harvard used the IMP-Teletype message convention or what we call 'IMP ASCII messages' (without marking) because it would allow them to use IMP-Teletypes for logging in and testing. Multics, on the other hand, used the standard network message format (with marking) to have Host-Host compatibility as per accepted protocols. Both approaches have merit. The IMP-Teletype message format should be changed to conform with the network standard -- it should have marking.

Finally, we would like to announce our readiness to participate in experiments which will further extend our confidence and competence in networking, especially experiments which, like the preceding, will have very large returns with relatively small investment.

Roster of those participating

Ben Barker	Harvard, BBN
Grenville Bingham	MITDG
Howard Brodie	MITDG
Dan Cohen	Harvard
Tom Knight	MITDG, MIT/AI
John McQuillan	Harvard
Bob Metcalfe	MITDG, Harvard
Ed Meyer	Multics
Mike Padlipsky	Multics
Tom Skinner	Multics
Ed Taft	Harvard

About the Author

Just a few hours after finishing this doctoral dissertation, on May 22, 1973 at the Xerox Palo Alto Research Center, Bob Metcalfe wrote a memo inventing Ethernet, the local-area networking (LAN) technology. In 1979, to promote Ethernet as an international standard for personal computer LANs, Metcalfe founded 3Com Corporation, the Fortune 500 global data networking company from which he retired in 1990. There are now 50 million computers on Ethernets worldwide.

In 1980, Metcalfe received the Association for Computing Machinery (ACM) Grace Murry Hopper Award, and in 1988, the Institute of Electrical and Electronics Engineers (IEEE) Alexander Graham Bell Medal, both for his leadership in the invention, standardization, and commercialization of Ethernet. In 1995, Metcalfe received the San Francisco Exploratorium Public Understanding of Science Award, his first in journalism, and was elected to the American Academy of Arts and Sciences. In 1966, Metcalfe was awarded the IEEE Medal of Honor.

Metcalfe received two bachelor of science degrees in 1969 after five years at the Massachusetts Institute of Technology, in electrical engineering and in management. From Harvard University, he received a master of science degree in applied mathematics in 1970 and a Ph.D. in computer science in 1973.

While working in Silicon Valley at Xerox (1972–1979) and 3Com (1979–1990), Metcalfe was also Consulting Associate Professor of Electrical Engineering at Stanford University where he taught distributed computing (1975–1983).

Today, Metcalfe writes a weekly column in the Internet section of InfoWorld. He is Vice President for Technology of InfoWorld's parent, International Data Group (IDG), which publishes computer magazines in 70 countries. He also serves on the Executive Committee of MIT's Board of Trustees.

Metcalfe lives with his family on a rare-breed sheep farm in Maine. He welcomes electronic mail over the Internet at bob_metcalfe@infoworld.com.

Other books in the "Computer Classics Revisited" Series

Code and Commentary on the UNIX Operating System (V6)

John Lions
Hardcover • $39.95 • ISBN 1-57398-013-7

At last you can purchase a non-photocopied version of the most important UNIX book never (before!) published. Written in 1977 at the University of New South Wales, Lions' underground classic gives the complete source code to Version 6, and also provides a brilliant exposition worthy of the spare, elegant code he describes. Forewords by Dennis Ritchie and Michael Tilson, with retrospective essays by Mike O'Dell, Peter Reintjes, Berny Goodheart, Greg Rose, and Peter Collinson.

Planning the ARPANET: The BBN Reports for 1969

Bolt Beranek & Newman
Hardcover • $39.95 • ISBN 1-57398-014-5

In December 1968 the Advanced Research Projects Agency awarded a 14-month contract to Bolt Beranek & Newman for the first-ever heterogeneous computer network. That network of four sites (UCLA, SRI, UCSB, the University of Utah) has evolved into the 50-million host Internet. Here, for the first time in print, are the four 1969 BBN technical reports that describe the construction and development of the ARPANET from project commencement to the connection of the first imp. Foreword by Dave Walden, ARPANET team member and former VP of BBN, who experienced it all.

Before the ARPANET: RFCs 1-10 + "A Study of Computer Network Design Parameters" (SRI)

Hardcover • $39.95 • ISBN 1-57398-008-0

In December 1967 the ARPA Network Working Group awarded SRI the contract to study "the design and specification of a computer network." Over the next few months Elmer Shapiro circulated a number of notes and suggestions which culminated in this landmark report, which presented the model ARPANET which was then implemented by BBN. Also in this Volume—RFCs 1 through 10, never-before available in print (and not available electronically). Introduction by Peter H. Salus, Series Editor and author of *Casting the Net: From ARPANET to Internet and Beyond* (1995).

Other fine books by Peer-to-Peer Communications

Ethernet Configuration Guidelines

Charles Spurgeon
156 pages • $19.95 • ISBN 1-57398-012-9

Ethernet works with a huge variety of media types; specifications are scattered throughout a mass of IEEE's 802.x standards. These guidelines overcome the complexity and bring all the configuration rules together in a single, convenient reference (includes 100Base-T "Fast Ethernet"). Anyone who administers, installs, supports, or designs Ethernet LAN's will appreciate this practical, hands-on professional quick reference.

Operating System Source Code Secrets Series

Volume 1: *The Basic Kernel Source Code Secrets* **William F. Jolitz &**
Lynne Greer Jolitz 550 pages • $49.95 • ISBN 1-57398-026-9
Volume 2: *Virtual Memory Source Code Secrets* **William F. Jolitz &**
Lynne Greer Jolitz Available early 1996 • ISBN 1-57398-027-7

One of Berkeley UNIX's lead developers teaches the inner workings of modern, high-performing operating systems (e.g. Windows NT, UNIX, Mach) via complete line-by-line source code annotations. Based on a port of Berkeley UNIX, with advanced non-UNIX features added, profiled in a 17-part *Dr. Dobb's Journal* serialization.

The PCMCIA Software Developer's Handbook

Dana L. Beatty, Steven M. Kipisz and Brian E. Moore
335 pages • $49.95 • ISBN 1-57398-010-2

Foreword by the chairman of the PCMCIA technical committee, 1990-1993. A comprehensive treatment of programming and debugging PC Card devices. Covers the new 1995 PC Card Standard. Includes a diskette containing program templates, utilities, and other development aids. The authors are IBM's project lead and staff programmers responsible for PCMCIA implementation for PowerPC.

The Computer Consultant's Workbook

Janet Ruhl
288 pages • $39.95 • ISBN 0-9647116-0-5

A nuts-and-bolts guide to navigating the computer consulting minefields, providing sample documents (e.g. contracts, letters), telemarketing scripts, tax and legal problem areas, and other vital topics. The author is a Sysop on CompuServe's Consultant's Forum.

The Politics of Information Management

Paul A. Strassmann
560 pages • $49.95 • ISBN 0-9620413-4-3

"Although it's modeled after Machiavelli's *The Prince*…Strassmann's book reflects the views of a Jeffersonian democrat, advising readers on how to apply democratic principles to the management of information to survive corporate politics."—*Information Week*. Paul Strassmann is corporate America's best-known authority on information systems management. *The Politics of Information Management* is a wonderful compendium of anecdotes and sage advice dealing with the organizational effects of computer technology (such as downsizing, reengineering, and turf battles!).

The Internet Joke Book

Brad Templeton
220 pages • $9.95 • ISBN 1-57398-025-0

This is a "best of the best" collection of eight years of electronic joke distribution on rec.humor.funny, the USENET newsgroup read daily by over 500,000 people world-wide. **Templeton**, publisher of the ClariNet on-line news service, edited rec.humor.funny for many years. Jokes cover sex, politics, religion, current events, celebrities, "things that never happen on Star Trek", 100+ light bulb jokes…and lots of programming humor.

For more information on these and other Peer-to-Peer books, contact your local bookstore, or email the publisher at info@peer-to-peer.com.

Peer-to-Peer Communications   Phone:(800) 420-2677
P.O. Box 640218   (408) 435-2677
San Jose, CA 95164-0218   Fax: (408) 435-0895